TRUST
YOUR
VIBES

GUIDED JOURNAL

TRUST YOUR VIBES

GUIDED JOURNAL

Reclaim the Missing Piece and
Access Your Intuition in
5 Minutes a Day

SONIA CHOQUETTE

HAY HOUSE

Carlsbad, California • New York City
London • Sydney • New Delhi

Published in the United Kingdom by:
Hay House UK Ltd, The Sixth Floor, Watson House,
54 Baker Street, London W1U 7BU
Tel: +44 (0)20 3927 7290; Fax: +44 (0)20 3927 7291; www.hayhouse.co.uk

Published in the United States of America by:
Hay House Inc., PO Box 5100, Carlsbad, CA 92018-5100
Tel: (1) 760 431 7695 or (800) 654 5126
Fax: (1) 760 431 6948 or (800) 650 5115; www.hayhouse.com

Published in Australia by:
Hay House Australia Ltd, 18/36 Ralph St, Alexandria NSW 2015
Tel: (61) 2 9669 4299; Fax: (61) 2 9669 4144; www.hayhouse.com.au

Published in India by:
Hay House Publishers India, Muskaan Complex, Plot No.3, B-2,
Vasant Kunj, New Delhi 110 070
Tel: (91) 11 4176 1620; Fax: (91) 11 4176 1630; www.hayhouse.co.in

A catalogue record for this book is available from the British Library.

Tradepaper ISBN: 978-1-83782-119-8

This product uses papers sourced from responsibly managed forests. For more information, see www.hayhouse.co.uk.

Printed and bound by CPI Group (UK) Ltd, Croydon CR0 4YY

"Always and in all ways,
trust your vibes."

— Sonia

CONTENTS

INTRODUCTION

After teaching people worldwide for over 50 years how to develop and strengthen their intuitive muscles and find a deeper sense of well-being and peace, I've realized that the biggest challenge isn't that people are not intuitive but rather that most are in the habit of ignoring this incredible, natural superpower, thus losing out on its invaluable guidance and benefits.

The remedy for this self-defeating tendency is simple: notice and write down what you intuitively feel every day. In a short time, you'll have evidence that your intuition is worth listening to—thus you will begin to pay attention to your intuition and put it to work as it is designed to do. This is how the idea for this *Trust Your Vibes Guided Journal* was born.

By writing in this journal for only a few minutes a day, in no time, you will have undeniable evidence that your intuition is reliable, trustworthy, and most importantly, essential to your well-being. Written by your own hand, this evidence will motivate you to begin trusting your vibes as you navigate through life. It will feel as though you are turning on a bright light in what otherwise was a very dark and scary world. More and more you will be able to intuitively sense the best steps forward. You will recognize obstacles before you encounter them, thus avoiding setbacks. You will start noticing opportunities, even when hidden, thus advancing yourself quickly. You will also feel more congruent, grounded, confident, and secure, thus improving your mental and physical well-being. When this happens, your life dramatically shifts from ordinary daily grind and struggle to extraordinary ease and flow. This is your natural design, and when your intuition is activated and engaged, what you dream in your heart becomes an accessible reality.

HOW TO USE THIS JOURNAL

This is a four-month daily journal.

Every morning, before you write anything, you will first be guided to shift your attention from your head to your heart and connect to your inner guidance. Make yourself comfortable. Look around. Get centered and gently close your eyes. Take a deep breath, slowly exhale, and smile. This will open your heart and directly connect you with your intuition.

Next, you will be given a brief prompt and asked a few questions designed to nudge your intuition into action. After writing down your answers, you will then be invited to apply your newly awakened intuitive perception to the day ahead.

In the evening, just before retiring, you will have another brief prompt and a few questions asking you to review your day and record your results from that day's practice.

The evening prompt helps you recognize the ways in which your intuition helped you that day, which is often overlooked. Taking a few minutes to answer the evening prompt will help you sleep better because you will be gathering evidence that you can count on from your inner guidance—your "vibes"—to take care of you in every way.

On the fourth day of each week, starting with the fourth week, you will be introduced to what is called a "vibe check," an intuitive scan, first of your body, then of your surroundings and people, and then of all events and circumstances of your life. This scan is easy to do and helps naturally integrate intuition into your decision-making process. In no time you will be intuitively vibe checking everything as a matter of course.

On the seventh day of each week you will be invited to review your progress for the week. This is an exciting entry because with it, you can clearly measure your growth and development from week to week and see firsthand the enormous benefits that reinstating intuition as the leading guide in your life brings about.

TIME COMMITMENT

The daily time commitment in working with this journal will be around 5 to 10 minutes. Because you are working with a natural sense, activating your intuition is not a time- or labor-intensive effort. Rather it is an entertaining and illuminating exercise in self-awareness, bringing with it immediate benefits, inner confidence, and outer synchronicities. The positive and transformative results you will get from activating your intuition are almost instantaneous. You will no longer feel as though you are fumbling in the dark, trying to find your way forward, hoping to avoid danger and pain, and hoping to survive. Like turning on the light in a darkened room, you will clearly sense and see what is going on around you, making it far easier to make the best decisions in all areas of your life.

THE BENEFITS

Your daily journaling commitment will create the habit of using your intuition in every aspect of life, just as you use your other senses, and as it is designed to be used. Day by day, your minimal effort will strengthen your intuition, and inform you of all the unseen or hidden aspects of circumstances and situations unfolding before you. Best of all, within days of beginning, your journal entries will offer invaluable evidence that will confirm, beyond any doubt, that your intuition is a highly reliable and *essential* source of guidance and one you need to succeed in everything in life. It will become clear that your intuition is the missing piece that you've needed to experience and navigate life at the highest level.

With this convincing evidence in hand, you'll quickly gain the confidence you need to become the leader of your life, no longer being pushed around by uncertainty and second-guessing, and scrambling for a sense of safety that using five senses alone brings about. In no time, your life will beautifully transform as well. Anxiety, stress, uncertainty, and fear will give way to confidence, creativity, peace of mind, and synchronistic flow. You will start to feel like you are the luckiest person you know because things will start falling into place better than you could have ever imagined. That is the magic of letting your sixth sense, your spirit, guide your life.

Reinstating your intuition is not a linear shift. It will bring about an exponential improvement in all aspects of your life. This is because your inner guidance system, your "vibes," is the missing piece and the healing component that improves everything. Once your spirit and intuition lead your life, life begins to flow.

You won't have to take my word for it, however. Work with the journal for two weeks and see for yourself. When you reread your own entries, you will be amazed at how much easier life is when using all your senses, instead of only the outer ones.

In fact, you will have so much evidence that trusting your vibes is the best choice you've ever made, you'll wonder how you ever got by without doing this all along. This journal will soon become one of your favorite books because it will be the story of your personal power and inner well-being blossoming into being. I promise.

WEEK 1 ∞

This week you'll learn how your inner guidance system is designed and what it needs from you to work well.

DAY

1

The first step in living an intuitively guided life is to recognize that we have six senses, not five. Your sixth sense is intuition, experienced through vibration or "vibes." Using this sense is natural and necessary for experiencing well-being in all areas of life. We all have vibes. Sadly, most people ignore their sixth sense, and consequently, get lost in life. The most creative and aware among us, however, know the importance of their intuition and trust their vibes. This guides them on their path and leads them to continual success. We all have a sixth sense. Using it is one of the most empowering choices you will ever make in life.

MORNING JOURNALING:

Are you openly intuitive, or do you keep it to yourself?

What are your main challenges in life today? What would you like your intuition to help you with?

_____

_____

_____

_____

_____

EVENING REFLECTION:

How much did you rely on your intuition today? How consistent were your vibes? Did you feel them occasionally? All the time? Hardly ever? What was the best thing that happened today?

_____

_____

_____

_____

_____

_____

_____

_____

Take a few deep breaths and relax. Intuition begins with being present.

INTUITIVE MESSAGE
You have six senses, and the sixth is the most important.

2

Your sixth sense is the first sense to develop and the most important sense, as it is the guiding light of your life. Emanating from your heart, it is the first organ in your body to be developed. It is the voice of your spirit, your authentic Self. It guides you in how to stay healthy and safe. It leads you to the relationships that best support your growth, well-being, and happiness, and away from those that harm you. It helps you express your power and creativity, and manifest success, prosperity, and satisfaction in life. It alerts you when you are in danger, as well as when you abandon or betray yourself, and when others do as well. It guides you to love, which is the highest, most healing vibration in the human experience. It helps you to speak your truth and to hear when others are or are not speaking theirs. It reveals the path ahead and away from danger and dead ends. It connects you to the higher realms of reality and divine support and blessings. It is your lifeline to your Self, your source, your Creator, God, and the Universe. Your sixth sense is the necessary lifeline to your healthiest, happiest, highest Self. It is the key to your well-being in every way. It is the missing piece of our makeup as humans, and the key to success in every aspect of our human journey. Without it, one will always feel something is off, missing. What is missing is the connection to who you really are.

MORNING JOURNALING:

How aware of your intuition are you generally? How much have your vibes influenced your decisions? Do you check with your intuition when making decisions? Or do you try to "figure things out"? Do you ever go against your inner guidance?

_____

_____

_____

_____

_____

_____

_____

EVENING REFLECTION:
Were you aware of your intuition today? What was the best thing
that happened to you today?

_____

_____

_____

_____

_____

_____

Take a few deep breaths and relax. Intuition begins with
being present.

INTUITIVE MESSAGE
Your sixth sense is the missing piece, and following
it is the source of your well-being.

DAY

3

You don't "think" vibes. You feel them. And not "feel" as in feeling an emotion, but "feel" as in sensing subtle energetic vibrations or signals that convey a more accurate understanding of what is happening in your life than what meets the eye or is presently evident.

MORNING JOURNALING:

Do you feel your vibes very often? Where in your body do you feel your vibes the most? Do you acknowledge your vibes or keep them to yourself?

EVENING REFLECTION:

Did your vibes help you today? What did you learn? What was the best thing that happened today?

_____

_____

_____

_____

_____

_____

_____

_____

_____

_____

_____

_____

_____

_____

_____

_____

When you finish writing, take a few deep breaths and relax.

INTUITIVE MESSAGE
Vibes are not thoughts. They are *feelings*.

DAY

4

Your vibes communicate like a satellite GPS radar centered in your heart. It helps you navigate the road ahead by sending you advance warnings and helpful directions as you go. These signals originate in your heart and radiate throughout your entire body and are felt when your attention is available. *Your vibes*—your inner GPS— is your superpower sense. It works perfectly. It is simply waiting for you to turn it on.

MORNING JOURNALING:

Are you aware that you can program your inner guidance to lead you to where you want to go? Have you ever asked your inner guidance to take the lead?

In what area would you like your vibes to help you today?

_____

_____

_____

_____

_____

_____

_____

EVENING REFLECTION:

Did you use your vibes today? How did they help you? What did you discover today? What was the best thing that happened?

_____

_____

_____

_____

_____

_____

When you finish writing, take a few deep breaths and relax.

INTUITIVE MESSAGE
Turn on your inner GPS.

DAY

5

Our physical body needs to meet its basic needs to be able to register subtle energy. The most important of these is breath. When we hold our breath or breathe shallowly, we go into "fight or flight" mode. In this mode we put up energetic protective barriers around our body. Breathing shallowly or holding our breath—or the combination of both—creates an inner state of anxiety, which causes us to be overreactive instead of proactive and miss our intuition. Take a deep breath now. Enjoy the refreshment it brings. Exhale with a loud sigh, and feel the stress melt from your body. And then notice how much more aware you are.

MORNING JOURNALING:

Take a few deep breaths in through the nose, and slowly exhale, as if you're blowing out candles. What difference does this make in how you feel right now?

Set your smartwatch to alert you once an hour. Take a breathing break when the alert goes off. Three deep breaths in. Three sighs of relief out. Then notice your vibes.

EVENING REFLECTION:

How aware were you of your breathing throughout the day? Did you catch yourself holding your breath today? Breathing shallowly? Did you take any breathing breaks?

_____

_____

_____

_____

_____

_____

_____

What was the best thing that happened to you today?

_____

_____

_____

_____

_____

_____

_____

When you finish writing, take a few deep breaths and relax.

INTUITIVE MESSAGE
Breathe.

· 15 ·

DAY

6

The second most important thing your body needs is water. You can instantly tell if you are dehydrated by pinching your skin. If it goes right back, you are well hydrated. If your skin stays folded, you are dehydrated, and your perception is lowered. We are made up of 60 percent water, and water is a conduit for intuitive energy. If you are dehydrated, this blocks the flow and release of energy in our bodies. Dehydration traps emotions, affects your mood, increases pain and stress in the body, and decreases awareness. We *need* water to function on every level, and it is essential for intuitive awareness. Set an alert on your smartphone today to drink one glass of room-temperature water an hour throughout the day.

MORNING JOURNALING:

How much water do you generally drink in a day? A lot? Occasionally? Never? Only when extremely thirsty? What do you drink throughout the day?

_____

_____

_____

_____

Set your smartwatch to alert you once an hour to drink a glass of water. Room temperature water is best. Cold water shocks your system, and the benefit is reduced. Then notice how much more intuitively aware you are today.

EVENING REFLECTION:

How much water did you drink today? Did you remind yourself to drink water? Were you more aware of your vibes at any point today? What was the best thing that happened today?

_____

_____

_____

_____

_____

_____

_____

_____

_____

_____

_____

_____

_____

_____

When you finish writing, take a few deep breaths and a drink of water. Then relax.

INTUITIVE MESSAGE
Drink water.

The third most important need, when it comes to helping your sixth sense function at its best, is fueling your body with healthy food. Without getting into a full diet overhaul (which is unnecessary), there are a few basics that will have a big impact on how well your intuition works. The first is that your body needs, along with water and breath, protein in the morning to fuel your brain and help your awareness wake up. The second is that your body thrives on green plants, so eating these is terrific for heightened awareness. These two food choices fuel your well-being and activate your inner guidance. If your body doesn't have proper fuel, your attention shuts down. Good food equals higher awareness. It's that simple.

MORNING JOURNALING:

What did you/will you eat for breakfast this morning?

_____

_____

Do you even eat breakfast?

_____

_____

Do you eat fast food? Processed food? Lots of sugar?

_____

Do you eat enough greens? Any greens?

_____

Do you notice how your awareness varies depending on what you eat?

_____

_____

_____

_____

_____

Today, eat protein, low sugar, and fresh greens. Then notice how much easier it is to notice your vibes.

EVENING REFLECTION:

Did you eat protein and greens today? Did you reach for sugar to keep going? Were you more aware of your vibes at any point today? Did you drink enough water? Did you remember to breathe? What was the best thing that happened to you today?

_____

_____

_____

_____

_____

_____

When you finish writing, take a few deep breaths and relax.

INTUITIVE MESSAGE
Protein, low sugar, and greens, please.

WEEK 2 ∞ This week you will meet your spirit and your barking dog/ego.

DAY

1

Noticing your vibes is like noticing stars. Stars are always in the sky, shining brightly, but we forget to look up, so we miss them. Once you see one star, you then notice another and another. Pretty soon, the entire Milky Way opens before your eyes. It was there all along. The same happens with your inner guidance. Normally, we are so stuck in our heads, we miss seeing the stars. In the same way, we also miss our vibes.

MORNING JOURNALING:

Notice your world. Look around the room. Pick out three separate things with three different textures that you've never noticed before. Name them aloud. Next, turn your attention inward and focus on your inner experience. Pay attention to how you feel inside. Can you describe it? Tense? Relaxed? Groggy? Alert? Do you often notice how your body feels, or do you tune it out? Write this all down.

Fill in the following:

This morning, I noticed . . .

_____

_____

_____

_____

And looking inside, I noticed . . .

_____

_____

_____

_____

Keenly notice details inside and out today. And remember to breathe.

EVENING REFLECTION:

What did you notice today that you hadn't noticed before? How did your vibes support you today? What was the best thing that happened to you today?
Quickly write down everything that comes to mind.

_____

_____

_____

_____

_____

_____

_____

Take a few deep breaths and relax.

INTUITIVE MESSAGE
Notice the subtle.

You have two channels of perception and awareness. The first is the voice of your ego (the voice in your head), and the second is the voice of your spirit (the voice in your heart). Albert Einstein described these two voices this way: "The intuitive mind is a sacred gift, and the rational mind is a faithful servant. Unfortunately, we have created a society that honors the servant and has forgotten the gift." Your ego, or rational mind (the voice in your head), is like your pet dog—a faithful companion to the spirit, your authentic Self, the source of your vibes and inner guidance (the voice in your heart.)

MORNING JOURNALING:

Imagine your ego, that voice in your head, is your pet—a barking dog that wants to support and protect you. Describe your barking dog/ego, your faithful servant to your spirit. What kind of dog is your ego? Picture its breeding, temperament, and the ways it tries to control things. What type of personality does your barking dog/ego have? Is yours a nervous Chihuahua, an aggressive pit bull, an assertive German shepherd, a rambunctious terrier, a temperamental dachshund? Is yours an energetic puppy or an old dog set in his ways? Is it a boisterous, loud dog or a lazy lapdog who lies about? Have fun describing your barking dog/ego.

My barking dog is named _____. He or she is (describe)

_____

_____

_____

_____

Read aloud what you've written. Be aware of your barking dog/ego today.

How aware of your barking dog/ego were you today? Did you encounter anyone else's barking dog/ego? Did it make you smile or annoy you to no end?

When you finish writing, take a few deep breaths and let your barking dog/ego know it's okay to relax.

INTUITIVE MESSAGE
Recognize your barking dog/ego.

DAY

3

As eager as your barking dog ego is to protect and guide you in life, it is incapable of doing a good job. This is because your ego, by nature, is a defensive, fearful, reactive animal that can easily misinterpret others and make poor decisions. We don't get rid of the barking dog/ego. That's impossible, nor is it necessary. The ego is designed to be your faithful servant, your helper. Therefore, all you need to do is train your barking dog/ego, so it knows how to help you best instead of trying to control everything. Nothing trains your barking dog/ego quite like meditation. It is the perfect way to calm your reactive nature, help your ego take a step back, and tune in to your heart and spirit, the true and capable leader of your life. Meditation calms your nerves, relaxes your mind, and sharpens your intuition. It doesn't take talent to meditate. It only takes patience, consistency, and reasonable expectations. The key is not to expect anything other than some peace and quiet for a few minutes every day to calm your barking dog/ego and connect with your spirit.

MEDITATION PRACTICE:

Here's an easy meditation practice:

Look around the room, and get comfortable. When you feel safe and at ease, close your eyes. Next, inhale to the count of four. Hold your breath to the count of four. Next, exhale to the count of four. Again, hold to the count of four. Repeat 10 times. Then smile. Eventually, as you get the hang of it, you repeat 20 times. That's it. It's that simple. And it works miracles if you meditate daily.

MORNING JOURNALING:

Do you meditate? Have you noticed any benefits, if you are presently meditating? What is your resistance, if any, on your part if you are not meditating? Write down your thoughts about meditation or your past experiences with meditation. How will meditation help you?

_____

_____

_____

_____

_____

Commit to meditating for 5 to 15 minutes every day for the next month. It's not a duty. It's a gift that keeps on giving.

EVENING REFLECTION:

Did you meditate today? Did your barking dog/ego try to run this show? How did your intuition support you today? What was the most fun you had today?
Quickly write down everything that comes to mind.

_____

_____

_____

_____

_____

Take a few deep breaths and relax.

INTUITIVE MESSAGE
Meditate daily.

DAY

4

Your spirit is not your ego or personality. Your spirit is the timeless, limitless, brilliant, loving, creative Divine essence that knows best how to take care of you. It speaks to you in your heart, and radiates outward, throughout your body. Your Spirit is the voice behind your vibes. It is the natural compass of your life.

MORNING JOURNALING:

Describe your spirit. You can meet your spirit in what you love, what lights you up, and in what gives you energy. You meet it where you get lost in having fun and lose all self-consciousness. Your spirit is you at your happiest and best. To help differentiate your spirit from your ego, give your spirit its own beautiful name. Choose a name that matches the feeling or the energy that your spirit reflects. Like Sunshine or Radiance. Don't allow your barking dog to get worked up about meeting your spirit. Ask your spirit, "What is your name?" and take the first thing that comes to mind. Enjoy this. Have fun. Don't worry about getting the name right. You can always change it later if you'd like. After all it is your spirit. My spirit is:

_____

_____

I name my spirit: (Quickly choose a name that makes you happy or springs to mind. Don't overthink.)

_____

Read aloud what you've written. Be aware of your spirit today.

Were you aware of your spirit today? What gifts did you receive today? What was the best thing that happened to you today?

_____

_____

_____

_____

_____

_____

_____

_____

_____

_____

_____

_____

_____

_____

_____

When you finish writing, take a few deep breaths and relax.

INTUITIVE MESSAGE
Be aware of your spirit.

DAY
5

Your spirit is your sacred, Divine, authentic Self. You connect with your spirit most profoundly when engaged in doing things you love. This is called being "in love," and you don't need a romantic partner to be "in love." When "in love" your barking dog/ego calms down and your spirit takes over. When "in love" your heart fully opens. When doing something you truly love, you are present, awake, aware, creative, engaged, peaceful, and in the flow. It is your ideal state of being. Even thinking about what you love awakens your spirit and overrides your barking dog/ego. When "in love" your spirit fills your body with energy and light. Your inner guidance becomes loud and clear, and your barking dog goes silent.

MORNING JOURNALING:

The quickest way to a become familiar with your spirit is to fill in the following:

I love _____.

I love _____.

I love _____.

I love _____.

I love _____.

I love _____.

I love _____.

I love _____.

Do as much of what you love today as possible. Notice how your spirit takes over your body when you do.

EVENING REFLECTION:

Did your spirit do anything you love today? Did your barking dog/ego support your spirit? Or did it compete with or attack your spirit? What challenged your barking dog/ego today? What was the best part of the day?

_____

_____

_____

_____

_____

_____

_____

_____

_____

_____

_____

_____

When you finish writing, take a few deep breaths and enjoy your spirit.

INTUITIVE MESSAGE
Do what you love.

DAY

6

Most people only pay attention to their five external senses and ignore their spirit and vibes. They tune out or deny the unseen world of energy, and instead are guided solely in life by their barking dog/ego. This is living from the *outside* in. An intuitive person, on the other hand, listens for the signals from their spirit and follows its beneficial guidance every day. They live from the inside out. This is our natural design, and the way life works best.

MORNING JOURNALING:

Do you live from the outside in or the inside out? Are you listening to your barking dog/ego or your spirit?

_____

What is your barking dog/ego yapping about today?

_____

Now focus on your heart and Spirit. What does your spirit (vibes) communicate?

_____

Today notice the difference between your barking dog/ego and your spirit.

EVENING REFLECTION:

Were you outside in or inside out today? What was your biggest challenge today? What input did your spirit offer? What was the best thing that happened today?

_____

_____

_____

_____

_____

_____

_____

_____

_____

_____

_____

_____

_____

_____

_____

When you finish writing, take a few deep breaths. Enjoy your spirit and encourage your barking dog/ego to relax.

INTUITIVE MESSAGE
Live from the inside out.

MORNING JOURNALING:

What was the most enlightening thing you learned this week?

_____

_____

_____

_____

_____

_____

Did you remember to breathe, drink water, and eat protein and greens?

_____

_____

_____

_____

_____

_____

Did you listen to your spirit? Do you struggle with your barking dog/ego?

_____

_____

_____

_____

What was your biggest challenge this week?

_____

_____

_____

_____

What was the best thing that happened?

_____

_____

_____

What was most fun this week?

_____

_____

_____

_____

INTUITIVE MESSAGE
Let your spirit lead.

DAY

1

If you want to accurately tune in to your vibes, it is necessary to be physically and emotionally grounded. If you are stressed, overwhelmed, and ungrounded, you won't be able to sense the subtle energy coming from your heart and spirit that will guide you forward to higher ground.

You are grounded if you are breathing calmly, if you are present and centered, and if you feel connected to the ground. You are ungrounded if you feel stressed, agitated, rushed, threatened, reactive, angry, or overwhelmed. Being grounded is essential to your well-being.

MORNING JOURNALING:

Do you generally feel grounded or ungrounded? Is there anyone or any situation that leaves you feeling emotionally stressed, anxious, fearful, threatened, or overwhelmed right now? Are you physically addressing your basic needs for food, water, sleep, and quiet? Do you feel pressured or unable to make clear decisions?

_____

_____

_____

_____

_____

_____

_____

_____

_____

_____

EVENING REFLECTION:

Did anything happen today that left you feeling ungrounded?
Were you able to stop, re-center, and get grounded once again?
How did your inner guidance help you today?
Quickly write down everything that comes to mind.

_____

_____

_____

_____

_____

_____

_____

_____

Take a few deep breaths and relax.

INTUITIVE MESSAGE
Get grounded.

DAY

2

Your body is a fantastic, intuitive radio receiver, designed to pick up and relay intuitive information, just as actual radio receivers are designed to receive and relay sound vibrations. Being open to intuition is the equivalent of turning "on" your inner radio receiver. This receives broadcast guidance from your spirit to help you gracefully navigate through the day. Nothing and no one does a better job.

MORNING JOURNALING:

Is your inner radio receiver turned on? Are you open to receiving intuitive guidance from your spirit? Or are you stuck in your head, listening to your noisy barking dog/ego? Answer honestly.

_____

_____

_____

_____

_____

_____

_____

_____

Keep your intuitive receiver on today.

EVENING REFLECTION:

How did your spirit help you today? What gifts did you receive? Were you able to follow your spirit, or did your barking dog/ego get in the way?

Quickly write down your response.

_____

_____

_____

_____

_____

_____

_____

_____

_____

_____

_____

_____

_____

_____

_____

Now take a few deep breaths and relax.

INTUITIVE MESSAGE
Be open to inner guidance.

DAY

3

While being open turns your intuition receiver on, expecting to sense or hear your intuition guides your attention directly to the broadcast of "your spirit." The more you expect your intuition to work for you, the more available you are to guidance. And the more guidance you will receive.

MORNING JOURNALING:

Do you *expect* your intuition to be available to you when you need it? When in the past have you needed inner guidance and received it?

_____

_____

_____

_____

_____

_____

_____

_____

_____

_____

Expect your intuition to guide you all day today.

EVENING REFLECTION:

Did you expect your intuition to help you today? What was the best part of your day? What unexpected blessing came through today? Quickly write down your response.

_____

_____

_____

_____

_____

_____

_____

_____

_____

_____

_____

_____

_____

_____

_____

When you finish writing, take a few deep, relaxing breaths, and release the day.

INTUITIVE MESSAGE
Expect your spirit to guide you.

4

Your vibes tune into the unseen world and alert you to information that your logical brain cannot perceive. That's why vibes are so valuable, and why it is important to listen to them. This can be challenging to your barking dog/ego when you do not have immediate evidence to support them. Just remember you do have a sixth sense that is working, so trust your vibes anyway. The evidence will come in time. If you do, you will avoid difficulties, roadblocks, even disasters lying ahead, while at the same time meeting with open doors, blessed opportunities, synchronicities, and divine support. Nothing lowers stress more than this.

MORNING JOURNALING:

Do I trust my vibes? Or do I second-guess my intuition, wasting time by figuring out why I intuitively feel what I do? Do I trust my spirit, or do I seek other people's opinions over my inner guidance?

_____

_____

_____

_____

_____

_____

_____

Read your answers aloud. Notice how they leave you feeling. Act on your intuition today.

EVENING REFLECTION:

What did I notice today that I hadn't before? How did my intuition
support me today? What was the best part of my day?
Quickly write down everything that comes to mind.

_____

_____

_____

_____

_____

_____

_____

_____

_____

_____

_____

_____

_____

Take a few deep breaths and relax.

INTUITIVE MESSAGE
Trust your vibes.

DAY

5

When you open to intuition, you turn on your intuitive receiver. When you expect intuition to guide you, you dial in to the bandwidth called your "vibes" or spirit. When you trust your intuition, you listen to its beautiful broadcast and let it sink in. When you act on your vibes, you let your guidance move you. Acting on your vibes is when they begin to make a transformational difference in your life.

MORNING JOURNALING:

Can you recall any moments when you acted on your intuition and had a positive outcome? Can you remember when you got stuck in your head, cornered by your barking dog/ego, and were afraid to follow your vibes even though you knew they were right? Are you getting more comfortable acting on your intuition since beginning this journal?

_____

_____

_____

_____

_____

_____

Feel the power and sovereignty that comes with acting on your vibes.

EVENING REFLECTION:

Did you act on your vibes today? (These don't have to be big deals. Reflect on little deals like looking in a particular place for your lost keys because your vibes told you to, and finding them.) How did your intuition support you today? What was the best part of your day?

Quickly write down everything that comes to mind.

_____

_____

_____

_____

_____

_____

_____

_____

_____

_____

_____

_____

_____

_____

Take a few deep breaths and relax.

INTUITIVE MESSAGE
Act on your vibes.

· 43 ·

DAY

6

Your spirit, your intuition, supports your priorities. These come in four categories: physical, emotional, mental, and spiritual. Physical priorities focus on your health, well-being, vitality, and safety. Mental priorities focus on creativity, responsibility, success, and security. Emotional priorities are concerned with relationships and personal intimacy and happiness. Spiritual priorities are concerned with your soul's growth, sense of purpose, contribution, and meaning in life. Establishing your priorities in these four areas gives your spirit direction in how to create the life you want.

MORNING JOURNALING:

Take a moment to consider what matters to you. Then fill in the following:

My top three physical priorities today are:

1 _____

2 _____

3 _____

My top three mental priorities today are:

1 _____

2 _____

3 _____

My top three emotional priorities are:

1 _____

2 _____

3 _____

My top three spiritual priorities are:

1 _____

2 _____

3 _____

Read aloud what you wrote and notice how these words resonate in your body. Do they feel true, congruent, and in alignment with your spirit? Listen to your vibes as they lead you in this direction today.

EVENING REFLECTION:

Were you able to focus on any of your priorities today, or did you get distracted? Did your vibes help today? What was the best thing that happened today?

_____

_____

_____

_____

When you finish writing, take a few deep breaths and relax.

INTUITIVE MESSAGE
First things first.

DAY

7

MORNING JOURNALING:

Did you establish your priorities?

_____

_____

_____

_____

Did you meditate daily? Drink enough water? Remember to breathe?

_____

_____

_____

_____

What was the most valuable thing you learned or discovered about yourself this week?

_____

_____

_____

_____

What was your biggest challenge this week?

_____

_____

_____

_____

_____

What was the best thing that happened this week?

_____

_____

_____

_____

Who was mostly in charge this week? Your spirit or your barking dog/ego?

_____

_____

_____

_____

_____

_____

INTUITIVE MESSAGE
Always trust your vibes.

DAY

1

Once you establish your priorities, the next step is to set your intentions. Setting your intentions puts focus and action into your priorities. Setting intentions reflects your commitment to taking full responsibility for your well-being and directing your life in the way you want it to go instead of being pushed around by others. You let your Sprit lead when you set your intentions. It informs your inner GPS where you want to go now.

MORNING JOURNALING:

List your top three intentions today:

1 _____

_____

2 _____

_____

3 _____

_____

Read aloud what you've written. Focus on these intentions today, and let your inner GPS guide you there.

EVENING REFLECTION:

Which intention did you focus on today? Is this a new intention, or have you had it for a while? How have your intentions changed, shifted, or evolved in the past three months?
Quickly write down the response.

_____

_____

_____

_____

_____

_____

_____

_____

_____

_____

_____

_____

_____

When you finish, take a few deep breaths. Relax and focus on what is important right now, which, at the end of the day, is to rest.

INTUITIVE MESSAGE
Set your intentions.

DAY

2

Nothing blocks inner guidance and destabilizes your well-being more than fear because it closes the heart, the source of our inner guidance. Some fears make sense, like the fear of walking into traffic or the fear of putting your hand on a hot stove, because these are things that clearly put you in danger and cause you pain. However, it is the vague fear of things like being vulnerable, feeling rejected, making a mistake, being out of control, or feeling unwanted that block our inner guidance and keep our barking dog/ego working overtime to protect us. The good news is that you don't have to overcome fears to be intuitively guided. You simply must acknowledge you are afraid instead of hiding it. Once you recognize you are fearful and of what, you bring your fear into the light, and your heart reopens. This allows your intuition to separate real danger from imagined threats. This keeps you out of danger and gets you back into the flow. You'll feel better immediately.

MORNING JOURNALING:

What fears are you hiding today? Some may be more obvious than others, so dig deep and try to bring everyone into the light.
I'm afraid of _____.

_____

_____

_____

_____

Trust your vibes today, and breathe into your fears.

EVENING REFLECTION:

Did your vibes help address and relieve your fears today? What was the best part of your day?
Quickly write down everything that comes to mind.

_____

_____

_____

_____

_____

_____

_____

_____

_____

_____

_____

_____

_____

_____

_____

Take a few deep breaths and relax.

INTUITIVE MESSAGE
Bring your fear into the open.

3

Following your intuition doesn't make you a "weirdo." It makes you a conscious, aware, and empowered person. A fear of being perceived as a "weirdo" by others is often a hangover from childhood, when being different from your peers risked ostracism and ridicule. Don't let what happened in middle school keep you from owning your superpower today.

MORNING JOURNALING:

Were you ever considered a "weirdo" for being intuitive? Have you ever been called a "weirdo" or been rejected by others because you are intuitive? Do you hide your intuition or water it down for fear of being perceived as a weirdo? *Do you think you're a "weirdo" because you're intuitive?*

_____

_____

_____

_____

_____

_____

_____

Lean into being a "weirdo" and enjoy it. This means you don't need others' approval any longer. It's very freeing.

EVENING REFLECTION:

What did I notice today that I hadn't before? How did my intuition support me today? What weird thing happened today? What was the best part of my day?
Quickly write down everything that comes to mind.

_____

_____

_____

_____

_____

_____

_____

_____

_____

_____

_____

_____

_____

_____

_____

Take a few deep breaths and relax.

INTUITIVE MESSAGE
"Weirdo" is the way to go.

DAY

4

A vibe check is a basic intuitive tool that will help you energetically scan anything and everything in your life, giving you clear insight that your five physical senses miss. You will start doing a vibe check in your body, gaining insight and information about the unseen world and how it is affecting you. Once you get comfortable with a basic vibe check, you will move on to vibe checking specific things like places, people, even upcoming events, and more. Eventually a vibe check will be second nature. You will come to use your intuitive sixth sense to energetically assess everything in your life, leaving you calm, grounded, informed, and guided, in all situations, so you feel peaceful and secure.

MORNING VIBE CHECK:

To begin, take a deep breath through the nose, and then exhale, as if you're blowing out candles, and with it, completely empty everything you are holding on to or that is holding on to you. Repeat this a few times or until your mind feels empty and quiet.

Once you complete this step, close your eyes, turn your attention inward, and slowly scan your body, starting at the feet and moving up to your crown. As you scan each area of your body, see if you sense any subtle energy trying to get your attention. Don't intellectualize or overthink. Simply notice and trust everything you spontaneously sense or feel, however subtle, and trust what comes to mind when you notice it.

When you do sense something, stop, and, like a curious detective, ask the following questions:

"What is this?" "Who is this?" "What is this about?" "What message do you have for me?"

Answer quickly with the first thing that enters your mind. Don't try to be logical or justify what you feel, because you won't be able to. Simply trust what spontaneously shows up, knowing these are your vibes talking, not your logical brain. Believe it or not, this works.

Your vibe check revealed:

_____

_____

_____

_____

_____

_____

When you have finished writing, read aloud what you've recorded. Stop and occasionally vibe check as you move through your day.

EVENING REFLECTION:

What did you discover when vibe checking today?
Quickly write your response.

_____

_____

_____

_____

_____

When you are finished writing, fully relax.

INTUITIVE MESSAGE
Vibe check everything and often.

DAY

5

Intuition is the act and art of tuning into subtle energy. This is challenging if you are disorganized, chaotic, and out of order. The more organized your life is, the easier it will be to notice intuitive vibes and put them to work for you.

MORNING JOURNALING:

How organized are you? Where do you feel most disorganized? What interferes most with your ability to focus and be organized?

_____

_____

_____

_____

To get organized today, answer the following:
What are your top three goals today?

1 _____

_____

2 _____

_____

3 _____

_____

_____

Stay focused on these three intentions today. Life organizes best around your focused commitments.

EVENING REFLECTION:

What did you intuitively notice today that you hadn't before? Were you able to organize your day around your top three priorities? Quickly write down everything that comes to mind.

_____

_____

_____

_____

_____

_____

_____

_____

_____

_____

_____

_____

Take a few deep breaths and relax.

INTUITIVE MESSAGE
Intuition thrives on order.

DAY

6

Holding on to old, outgrown, and unnecessary physical and emotional baggage blocks new energy from entering and makes it difficult to intercept subtle intuitive guidance. Periodic purges are an excellent way to help you stay in the flow, better attune to your intuition in present time, and get a breath of fresh air.

MORNING JOURNALING:

Is it time for a purge? What physical stuff needs to go? What old business, resentments, attitudes, stories, and agendas is it time to release? (Dig deep into the recesses of your heart and mind and let the old go.)

_____

_____

_____

_____

_____

_____

_____

_____

_____

_____

Read aloud what you've written. Do you notice any relief when decluttering your body and mind of old attitudes and resentments?

EVENING REFLECTION:

What do you need to let go of? What did you let go of today? How did your intuition support you today? What was the most joyful or happy part of the day?
Quickly write down everything that comes to mind.

_____

_____

_____

_____

_____

_____

_____

_____

_____

_____

_____

_____

_____

Take a few deep breaths and relax.

INTUITIVE MESSAGE
Declutter mind, body, and spirit.

7

MORNING JOURNALING:

Did you drink enough water this week? Eat your greens? Remember to breathe? Meditate?

_____

_____

_____

_____

What did you learn from your vibe check?

_____

_____

_____

_____

What old stuff needs to go?

_____

_____

_____

_____

In what area of life might you get better organized? Your physical space? Your time commitments? Establishing your priorities?

_____

_____

_____

_____

_____

Did you listen to your spirit or get chased by your barking dog/ego?

_____

_____

_____

_____

_____

What was the biggest blessing you received this week?

_____

_____

_____

_____

_____

_____

INTUITIVE MESSAGE
Always trust your vibes.

DAY

1

The more you connect with your spirit and begin to trust your vibes, the less distracted in the outer world you will be. Eventually you will find yourself needing or wanting less material stuff, as well as being less inclined to waste time on people who bring you down. You want to simplify your life, protect your time and energy, and focus more on who and what you love. You become eager to release everything that isn't compatible with your spirit.

MORNING JOURNALING:

Have you felt the urge to simplify your life in any way? Have your priorities changed since beginning this journey? Do you find yourself less interested in accumulating material things that have no real or lasting value? Have you noticed any change in how you wish to spend your time and with whom?

Notice your desire to simplify as you become even more aligned
with your spirit.

EVENING REFLECTION:

What was the best part of your day? Was your day complicated, or
were you able to keep it simple?

_____

_____

_____

_____

_____

_____

_____

_____

_____

_____

_____

_____

_____

When you finish writing, take a few deep breaths and exhale.

INTUITIVE MESSAGE
Keep it simple.

2

Your spirit constantly guides you to align with your authentic Self, and move toward all that creates a fulfilling, healthy, secure, and joyful life. Your spirit can only help, however, if you want to align with your true Self and move in the direction of what you love in life instead of fight against it.

MORNING JOURNALING:

What do you love most right now?

_____

_____

_____

_____

What would you love to experience today?

_____

_____

_____

Now focus on your heart and spirit. What do your vibes say?

_____

_____

_____

_____

EVENING REFLECTION:

How did your vibes help you today? What did you love most today?
What took you away from what you love today?

_____

_____

_____

_____

_____

_____

_____

_____

_____

_____

_____

_____

_____

_____

_____

_____

When you finish writing, take a few deep breaths and relax.

INTUITIVE MESSAGE
Align with your spirit.

DAY
———
3

We receive intuitive vibes through our body. They are physical but subtle. When we start to pay attention, we sense our vibes more clearly. They don't show up the same way in all people, nor do they show up in the same way in us all the time. For example, one moment you may get a gut feeling, or the hairs on your arms or at the back of your neck may stand up. At another moment, you might feel a subtle warmth in your heart, or a tingling in your throat, even a ringing tone in your ears. Your vibes are easy to miss if you're stuck in your head. When that happens, you become numb to these subtle signals. Being in your body is the beginning of more conscious, intuitive living.

MORNING JOURNALING:

How do your vibes capture your attention? Where in your body do you feel your vibes most often? Heart? Gut? Allover tingling? Light waves in the chest? Describe your vibes as clearly as you can.

_____

_____

_____

_____

_____

_____

Be aware of your vibes throughout the day.

EVENING REFLECTION:

Were you aware of your vibes at any point today? Now that you were made more keenly aware of them, were they any stronger than they might have been before? What was the best thing that happened today?

_____

_____

_____

_____

_____

_____

_____

_____

_____

_____

_____

_____

_____

_____

_____

When you finish writing, take a few deep breaths and relax.

INTUITIVE MESSAGE
Notice your vibes.

4

MORNING VIBE CHECK:

It is time, once again, to vibe check. This time, vibe check the space around you. It can be a home, an entire building, or any location that you may enter, work in, or visit today. You decide.

To begin, take a deep breath through the nose, and then exhale, as if you're blowing out candles, and with it, completely empty everything you are holding on to or that is holding on to you. Repeat this a few times or until your mind feels empty and quiet.

Once you complete this step, close your eyes, and imagine you are looking at a movie screen about 45 degrees above eye level. Call to mind the space you want to vibe check, and project it onto the screen. Once it is clear, just as you did with your body, slowly scan the space you selected, starting at the floor, and moving up to the ceiling. Then scan left to right of the space, followed by a front-to-back scan. As you scan each area of your space, notice the tone, weight, feeling, and overall energy. Don't intellectualize or overthink. Simply notice and trust everything you spontaneously sense or feel, however subtle, and trust what comes to mind.

When you sense something, stop, and, like a detective, ask the following questions:

"Who is this?" "What is this about?" "What do I need to know while in this space?"

Answer quickly with the first thing that enters your mind. Don't try to be logical or justify what you feel, because you won't be able to. Trust what spontaneously comes to mind, knowing your vibes will reveal the truth.

Your space vibe check revealed:

_____

_____

Vibe check various places you enter today, such as your office, a business building, someone's home, a store, even a restaurant, as you move through your day. Practice as much as you can, and try to notice the feeling of each place instead of the things inside the places.

EVENING REFLECTION:

Did you vibe check a place today? Which places did you vibe check? Your office? A restaurant? A store? What did your vibes reveal?

_____

_____

_____

_____

What did you love most about your day?

_____

_____

_____

Quickly write down everything that comes to mind.

_____

_____

_____

_____

Take a few deep breaths and relax.

INTUITIVE MESSAGE
Vibe check everything and often.

DAY

5

As spiritual beings, we are naturally born with a direct connection to our Creator, the Universe, as our source. For some, unfortunately, past religious indoctrination cut you off from directly connecting with your spirit, your source, and asked you to give away your power to controlling outside forces. This is the cause of some of our deepest inner malaise and goes against our natural design. If you want to feel peaceful, grounded, and guided at the deepest level, it's time to reconnect to your Divine source directly, through your heart and spirit.

MORNING JOURNALING:

As a child, was it ever suggested that your inner guidance wasn't a good thing? Have your beliefs evolved? Describe the kind of god or universal consciousness you connect with today.

_____

_____

_____

_____

_____

_____

_____

Today, keep your connection to Spirit free of others' opinions, beliefs, or control. Let your spirit speak directly to you, without interference from anyone or anything.

EVENING REFLECTION:

Did you feel a direct connection with your spirit and the Universe today? Were you subjected to religious training that caused you to doubt your inner guidance? Are you ready to take your power back and reconnect directly to Source? How did your vibes help you today?
Quickly write down everything that comes to mind.

_____

_____

_____

_____

_____

_____

_____

_____

_____

_____

Take a few deep breaths and relax.

INTUITIVE MESSAGE
Directly connect with your Creator and Source (the Universe).

6

One of the biggest reasons people tune out their natural inner guidance is because it points out what their egos do not want to hear. Sadly, many people prefer to believe what isn't true or cling to what isn't working instead of honestly looking at their life. Everyone knows in the long run this doesn't work. Trusting your vibes requires taking an honest look at things, even when this is difficult. You won't ever feel good if you're denying what you know in your heart to be true.

MORNING JOURNALING:

Is there anything your vibes tell you that you've been ignoring or denying because it makes you uncomfortable to admit or acknowledge?

How does acknowledging uncomfortable vibes from your spirit leave you feeling right now?

Name one uncomfortable vibe you've been ignoring.

Today, be willing to listen to your vibes even when they point out something you don't want to hear.

EVENING REFLECTION:

Are you available to the truth? How did your intuition support you today? What was the best part of the day?
Quickly write down everything that comes to mind.

_____

_____

_____

_____

_____

_____

_____

_____

_____

_____

_____

_____

_____

_____

_____

Take a few deep breaths and relax.

INTUITIVE MESSAGE
Denial is no protection.

7

MORNING JOURNALING:

Did you regularly meditate for a few minutes this week? Drink enough water? Breathe? What was the most valuable thing you learned or discovered about yourself this week?

_____

_____

_____

_____

_____

_____

_____

What was the biggest obstacle to trusting your vibes?

_____

_____

_____

_____

_____

_____

_____

How is trusting your vibes making a difference in your life so far?

_____

_____

_____

_____

_____

_____

_____

_____

_____

_____

_____

_____

_____

_____

_____

_____

_____

What were the biggest blessings you received this week?

INTUITIVE MESSAGE
Always trust your vibes.

DAY

1

Intuition works best when your heart is open. Our heart naturally opens when we are grateful in life. The more grateful we are, the higher our vibration, the more open your heart. And the more receptive to subtle energy and guidance you become. An open heart is a receptive heart. It is the healthiest heart, both physically and emotionally.

MORNING JOURNALING:

Write down everything you are currently thankful for. Consider blessings both big and small. Next, find three things in the most challenging areas in your life for which you can be thankful.

Keep your heart open, and freely express gratitude today.

EVENING REFLECTION:

What did you notice today that you hadn't before? Where's your heart open today? How did your vibes' intuition support you today? What was the best part of your day?
Quickly write down everything that comes to mind.

_____

_____

_____

_____

_____

_____

_____

_____

_____

_____

_____

_____

_____

_____

Take a few deep breaths and relax.

INTUITIVE MESSAGE
Open your heart.

DAY

2

Intuition sends vibrations throughout your body, even through your skin, all the time. These intuitive messages are experienced as "gut feelings," "hunches," "lightbulbs going off in your head," "ears ringing," and more. These subtle signals are trying to move you in the direction of your highest good. Every vibe is worth paying attention to.

MORNING JOURNALING:

Have you experienced any gut feelings, heart whispers, hits, hunches, or subtle feelings on any matter that you haven't fully acknowledged? Take a moment to be quiet and reflect on this question. Has any intuitive feeling slipped by recently? Write them all down here.

_____

_____

_____

_____

Do any of these feelings become stronger when you acknowledge them? Be specific.

_____

_____

_____

_____

EVENING REFLECTION:

How did your vibes support you today? What was your best intuitive insight today? Are you paying attention?
Quickly write down everything that comes to mind.

_____

_____

_____

_____

_____

_____

_____

_____

_____

_____

_____

_____

_____

_____

_____

_____

Take a few deep breaths and relax.

INTUITIVE MESSAGE
It all counts.

DAY

3

Trusting your vibes takes fortitude because often people around you may disapprove, dismiss, or discredit what you say. All of these are attempts to keep you from being empowered or to keep themselves from self-reflecting. In either case, ignore the negative feedback of others. Having the fortitude to be yourself and withstand these negative influences gives you confidence to navigate life in an honest and empowered way. It leaves you feeling authentic.

MORNING JOURNALING:

What is your greatest challenge in trusting your vibes? Who or what discourages you from trusting your inner guidance? Have you faced disapproval for your vibes in the past? Do you fear disapproval now? To what degree? A lot? A little?

_____

_____

_____

_____

_____

_____

Read aloud what you've just written. Then take a breath and exhale. Today, be courageous.

EVENING REFLECTION:

What did you notice today that you hadn't before? How did your vibes support you today? What was the best part of your day? Quickly write down everything that comes to mind.

_____

_____

_____

_____

_____

_____

_____

_____

_____

_____

_____

_____

_____

_____

Take a few deep breaths and relax.

INTUITIVE MESSAGE
Be courageous.

DAY

4

MORNING VIBE CHECK:

Today, vibe check your workspace.

To begin, take a deep breath through the nose, and then exhale, as if you're blowing out candles, and with it, completely empty everything you are holding on to or that is holding on to you. Repeat this a few times or until your mind feels empty and quiet.

Once you complete this step, close your eyes, turn your attention inward, and imagine you are looking at a movie screen about 45 degrees above eye level. Call to mind the space you want to vibe check, and project it onto the screen. Look at this inner screen, and slowly scan your office or working area, starting at the floor, and moving up to the ceiling. As you scan the area, (including closets and storage spaces if applicable), sense any subtle energy that reveals more than what meets the eye. Don't intellectualize or overthink. Simply notice everything you spontaneously sense or feel, however subtle, and acknowledge what comes to mind.

When you sense something, stop, and ask the following questions:

"Does this energy help or impede the flow at work?" "Does this energy have good vibes or not?" "How can I best clear the heavy energy from my working space? With a good cleaning? By opening windows, or changing the decor?"

Answer quickly with the first thing that enters your mind. Don't try to be logical or justify what you feel, because you won't be able to. Just trust what spontaneously comes to mind, knowing your body tells the truth.

Your office vibe check revealed:

_____

_____

Stop and occasionally vibe check the space wherever you are as you move through your day.

EVENING REFLECTION:

What did you notice today in your workspace when you did the vibe check? How can you best bring good vibes to the space where you work?
Quickly write down everything that comes to mind.

_____

_____

_____

_____

_____

_____

_____

_____

_____

_____

_____

_____

Take a few deep breaths and relax.

INTUITIVE MESSAGE
Vibe check everything and often.

DAY

——

5

Trusting your vibes requires patience because intuition often tunes in to either what is yet to be revealed or yet to happen. Both situations usually cannot be instantly verified. Keep this in mind, and be patient with your vibes, knowing your inner guidance will make sense in time. If others challenge you, don't argue. Simply say, "I trust my vibes. They work for me."

MORNING JOURNALING:

Reflect on the past few weeks.

Have you felt things for which you have no physical or sensory evidence yet? Have you ever felt things that made no logical sense but still rang true to you? When this occurred, did you listen and trust your vibes? Or did you deny or ignore them because you had no direct evidence to support them?

_____

_____

_____

_____

_____

_____

_____

Read aloud what you've just written. Then take a breath and focus inward. Notice how your intuition is getting stronger. Pray for patience. Continue to trust your vibes today.

What did you notice today that you hadn't before? How did your intuition support you today? What was the best part of your day? Did you have any fun today? If yes, what were you doing? Quickly write down everything that comes to mind.

Take a few deep breaths and relax.

INTUITIVE MESSAGE
Believe it.

DAY

6

Your intuition points out the most direct path to your safety, growth, emotional fulfillment, and sense of purpose. While your spirit will shine a light on your path through your intuition, you still must walk the path to get where you want to go.

MORNING JOURNALING:

How are your vibes communicating ways in which you can grow? What are your vibes revealing that supports your sense of purpose? Are you open to taking full responsibility for yourself? Is your intuition suggesting anything that you are reluctant to accept?

_____

_____

_____

_____

_____

_____

_____

_____

_____

Read aloud what you just wrote. Allow your spirit to guide you today.

EVENING REFLECTION:

In what areas of your life would you like to grow? How did your spirit support your growth today? Were you receptive to your intuition today, or did you tune it out?
Quickly write down everything that comes to mind.

_____

_____

_____

_____

_____

_____

_____

_____

_____

_____

_____

_____

_____

_____

Take a few deep breaths and relax.

INTUITIVE MESSAGE
Take responsibility for yourself.

DAY

7

TIME TO REVIEW

MORNING JOURNALING:

Did you meditate this week? Drink water? Breathe?

What was the most valuable thing you learned or discovered about yourself this week?

What is the biggest obstacle to trusting your vibes?

In what way were you challenged to grow?

_____

_____

_____

_____

_____

In what way has your intuition suggested something for which you did not receive outer support or agreement?

_____

_____

_____

_____

_____

What was your biggest blessing this week?

_____

_____

_____

_____

_____

INTUITIVE MESSAGE
Always trust your vibes.

DAY

1

The more consciously intuitive you become, the more your priorities and values will evolve with you. Therefore, it's helpful to review your priorities regularly so that inner guidance is operating with current instructions.

MORNING JOURNALING:

What are your top priorities today? How have they changed in the last few weeks? What does your inner GPS suggest now to help with your priorities and values?

_____

_____

_____

_____

_____

_____

Read aloud what you've written. Do your words resonate in your body? Are you making choices that support your priorities? Ask your inner guidance to help you accomplish your priorities today.

EVENING REFLECTION:

Have any priorities changed in the past few weeks? Did your vibes help you focus on your priorities today?
Quickly write down your response.

_____

_____

_____

_____

_____

_____

_____

_____

_____

_____

_____

_____

_____

_____

_____

_____

When you finish, take a few deep breaths and unwind.

INTUITIVE MESSAGE
Regularly update your priorities and values.

DAY

2

Your intuition is your best health insurance. It guides you in what is and is not good for your body, mind, and spirit. This includes the food you eat, the people you're around, the work you do, the places you go, and anything else that affects you in a day.

MORNING JOURNALING:

Have a conversation with your spirit and ask the following questions:

    What do I need to know about diet?

    What is my best exercise?

    How can I sleep better?

    How can I improve my overall health and vitality?

    What habits are keeping me from feeling good?

    What people are not good for my health?

Quickly write your responses, and don't let your barking dog/ego get in the way.

_____

_____

_____

_____

_____

_____

Read aloud what you've written. Follow this intuitive advice today instead of fighting or resisting, and see how you feel.

EVENING REFLECTION:

What did you learn today? What did your vibes say about how to take better care of your physical health? How did your intuition support you today? What was the best part of your day? Quickly write down everything that comes to mind.

_____

_____

_____

_____

_____

_____

_____

_____

_____

_____

_____

_____

_____

_____

Take a few deep breaths and relax.

INTUITIVE MESSAGE
Trust the feedback.

DAY

3

Clairvoyance is the intuitive ability to energetically sense beyond appearances, to sense the hidden truth of things and within people, with your inner eye or imagination. It literally means a "clear view."

MORNING JOURNALING:

Have you ever had a clairvoyant experience? Have you felt or "seen" past appearances and into people or situations? Have you ever clairvoyantly seen things that made you uncomfortable? Do you ever see into things or people in a way that reveals what someone is trying to hide?

What is your clairvoyance revealing now?

_____

_____

_____

_____

_____

_____

_____

_____

Pay attention to your clairvoyant insights today.

EVENING REFLECTION:

What did you clairvoyantly sense today? How did your intuition support you today? Where and with whom is your clairvoyance the strongest in your life? Is there anything you sense but don't want to see?
Quickly write down everything that comes to mind.

Take a few deep breaths and relax.

INTUITIVE MESSAGE
Get a clear view.

DAY

4

MORNING VIBE CHECK:

Today you will vibe check a specific person of your choice. This is not to spy on the person in a negative way. Your scan is to see if and how you can be of support to one another or to assure yourself that all is well with them and between you. For example, you can vibe check your kids, your partner, a good friend, a potential new business, a family member, or a potential partner. In other words, you can vibe check anyone you interact with in life.

To begin, take a deep breath through the nose, and then exhale, as if you're blowing out candles, and with it, completely empty everything you are holding on to or that is holding on to you. Repeat this a few times or until your mind feels empty and quiet.

Once you complete this step, close your eyes, turn your attention inward, and bring the person you want to vibe check forward into your imagination. Slowly scan their body and energy field as you did your own, starting from the feet and moving to the crown. As you scan the energy, look for any incongruities in their energy field, the space around them. Do you sense any subtle energy that draws your attention? Don't intellectualize or overthink. Simply notice everything you spontaneously sense or feel, however subtle, and trust what comes to mind.

When you sense something, stop, and say the following:

"What is this energy trying to communicate?" "Is there anything I need to know about this relationship or with this person?" "Please inform me on (fill in the subject of concern) regarding this person."

Answer quickly with the first thing that enters your mind. Don't try to be logical or justify what you feel, because you won't be able to. Just trust what spontaneously comes to mind, and write it down.

Your vibe check revealed:

_____

_____

_____

_____

_____

_____

When you have finished writing, reflect on what came into your awareness. If your vibe check was accurate, you will feel it throughout the day.

EVENING REFLECTION:

What did you discover when vibe checking a person today? Quickly write your response.

_____

_____

_____

_____

_____

When you are finished writing, relax, knowing we are all connected.

INTUITIVE MESSAGE
Vibe check everything and often.

DAY

5

If you feel bad vibes, or that something is "off," believe it, and don't waste time looking for explanations. In time, the source of your bad vibes will likely reveal itself. Walk away from bad vibes before they harm you. And if necessary, feel free to run.

MORNING JOURNALING:

Is there any area of your life or any person with whom you have bad vibes? Do you sense anything is "off" in any areas of your life or with any people in your life? How do you generally respond to bad vibes? Acknowledge any "off" or bad vibes you have now without needing an explanation.

_____

_____

_____

_____

_____

_____

_____

_____

Be especially alert when around situations or people who give you bad vibes. Don't stick around.

EVENING REFLECTION:

Meet with any bad vibes today? Are you sensing any bad or "off" vibes in general? Describe to the best of your ability what you are feeling about this person or situation.
What was the best part of your day?
Quickly write down everything that comes to mind.

_____

_____

_____

_____

_____

_____

_____

_____

_____

_____

_____

_____

_____

Take a few deep breaths and relax.

INTUITIVE MESSAGE
Quickly walk away from bad vibes.

DAY

6

Your inner guidance system looks for congruencies and flow in the energy field. When your intuition registers disturbances, it is because something is not in alignment with your spirit. Lies, dishonesty, misinformation, and manipulations, for example, even if delivered with a smile, create big disturbances in the energy field. This is energetic "BS" and "baloney." If you sense any of these conflicting energies coming from someone, (or from your barking dog/ego) your intuitive alarms will go off and let you know something is all wrong. Trust them.

MORNING JOURNALING:

Is there anyone in your life broadcasting incongruities? Is anyone gaslighting you, calling you "crazy" rather than admitting their own incongruities? Are you broadcasting energetic incongruities of your own, to yourself, or to others, saying something other than what is honest and true? Are you making decisions that leave you feeling aligned with your spirit? Or do they leave you feeling conflicted with yourself or others? Are you around anyone or any situation in which the energies don't match up with your spirit? What do your vibes say is really going on?

Read aloud what you've written. Pay attention to any vibrational incongruities today. Check to be certain they are not coming from you.

EVENING REFLECTION:

Did you encounter any energetic "BS" or "baloney" today? How did your intuition support you today? What was the best part of your day?
Quickly write down everything that comes to mind.

_____

_____

_____

_____

_____

_____

_____

_____

_____

_____

_____

_____

_____

_____

_____

Take a few deep breaths and relax.

INTUITIVE MESSAGE
Scrutinize the energy.

7

MORNING JOURNALING:

Did you meditate this week? Drink enough water? Eat your greens? Remember to breathe?

_____

_____

_____

_____

Did you feel aligned and congruent with your spirit, or did you fall out of alignment with yourself?

_____

_____

_____

_____

Did you encounter anyone whose energy felt incongruent or "off"?

_____

_____

_____

_____

_____

What was the most valuable thing you learned or discovered about yourself this week?

_____

_____

_____

_____

What are you most grateful for this week?

_____

_____

_____

_____

How is trusting your vibes improving your well-being?

_____

_____

_____

What was the biggest blessing you received this week?

_____

_____

_____

_____

INTUITIVE MESSAGE
Always trust your vibes.

DAY

1

Your spirit is constantly leading you to the most positive connections, creative opportunities, and soul-elevating experiences. Benefitting from these connections often involves making a change. Are you willing to do that?

MORNING JOURNALING:

Are your vibes encouraging you to try anything new? Is your intuition inviting you to change directions, enter a new or different area of work, relocate, or start a new business or creative project? What new things are your vibes inviting you to investigate? Are you open to exploring good vibes, or is your barking dog/ego chasing you away?

_____

_____

_____

_____

_____

_____

Follow your good vibes today.

EVENING REFLECTION:

What did you notice today that you hadn't before? Did you follow any good vibes lately? What was the best part of your day? Quickly write down everything that comes to mind.

_____

_____

_____

_____

_____

_____

_____

_____

_____

_____

_____

_____

_____

_____

_____

Take a few deep breaths and relax.

INTUITIVE MESSAGE
Be open to change.

DAY
2

When in alignment with your authentic spirit, your intentions, focus, and actions line up and move in the same direction. You enter a state of flow or grace. Life becomes a series of green lights guiding you directly toward your intentions without interference.

MORNING JOURNALING:

Have any green light vibes opened new doors of opportunity lately? Have you recently experienced a good vibe, hit, hunch, or gut feeling encouraging you to explore something new? Have you spontaneously felt called to move in any unexpected direction? Are you meeting with green lights?

_____

_____

_____

_____

_____

_____

_____

_____

Read aloud what you've written. Follow the intuitive green lights today.

Did you experience green light vibes today? How did your intuition support you? What was the best thing that happened today? Quickly write down everything that comes to mind.

_____

_____

_____

_____

_____

_____

_____

_____

_____

_____

_____

_____

_____

_____

Take a few deep breaths and relax.

INTUITIVE MESSAGE
Green light. Go!

3

What feels like being blindsided may be your spirit redirecting your life in a better way.

When everything seems to be lining up to move in one direction, and then it suddenly shifts, comes to a stop, or gets interrupted and moves another way that you didn't expect, know your spirit and the Universe have better plans for you.

MORNING JOURNALING:

Have you been blindsided, caught off guard, or thrown any curveballs in the past? Has anything in your life turned out to be other than what you had hoped or wished for, leaving you feeling ungrounded and insecure? Ask your spirit what you are meant to learn and how to best proceed. Quickly write the response below.

_____

_____

_____

_____

_____

_____

_____

_____

If you are blindsided by the unexpected, have no fear. Trust something better is on the way.

EVENING REFLECTION:

Were you dealt any curveballs lately? Did you meet with any surprising shifts or an unexpected turn of events? Did you have any surprises that caught you off guard? Check in with your vibes. Did you have any intuitive foresight?
Quickly write down everything that comes to mind.

_____

_____

_____

_____

_____

_____

_____

_____

_____

_____

_____

_____

_____

_____

Take a few deep breaths and relax.

INTUITIVE MESSAGE
The Universe has a better plan.

DAY

4

MORNING VIBE CHECK:

Today we will vibe check your job, career, or profession. To begin, take a deep breath through the nose, and then exhale, as if you're blowing out candles, and with it, completely empty everything you are holding on to or that is holding on to you. Repeat this a few times or until your mind feels empty and quiet.

Once you complete this step, close your eyes, turn your attention inward, and, using your imagination, slowly scan your work experience. As you scan each aspect of your work, see if you sense any subtle energy that captures your attention. Don't intellectualize or overthink. Simply notice and trust everything you spontaneously sense or feel, however subtle, and trust what comes to mind.

When you sense something, stop, and ask the following questions:

"What is this energy about?" "What do I need to know?" "What information do you have for me?"

Answer quickly with the first thing that enters your mind. Don't try to be logical or justify what you feel, because you won't be able to. Simply trust what spontaneously comes to mind, knowing this is how your intuition works.

Your vibe check revealed:

_____

_____

_____

_____

_____

_____

_____

_____

_____

When you have finished your vibe check, read aloud what you
wrote down. Let it sink in. Stop and occasionally vibe check as you
move through your day. Going forward, you can scan a present
work situation, or a future or desired work situation, at any time.

EVENING REFLECTION:

What did you discover when vibe checking today?
Quickly write your response.

_____

_____

_____

_____

_____

_____

_____

_____

When you are finished writing, fully relax.

INTUITIVE MESSAGE
Vibe check everything and often.

DAY

5

One of the best ways to activate your intuition is through your imagination. Every time you say, "I wonder . . . ," your imagination turns on the intuitive flow. By presenting "I wonder" questions to your spirit, your Higher Self, you step out of the logical brain and into your creative, intuitive brain, open to new possibilities.

MORNING JOURNALING:

Wonder about 10 things that you are curious about. This strengthens your intuitive muscles. Enter the world of imagination instead of intellectually trying to figure things out. Be curious without needing immediate answers. For example, "I wonder where I'll go on vacation this summer," or "I wonder who will visit me this year."

I wonder . . .

_____

_____

_____

_____

_____

_____

After you are done writing, read aloud what you've written. Give your brain, with its need to figure everything out, a break today, and have a wonder-filled day instead.

EVENING REFLECTION:

What was the most wonderful thing about today? How did your intuition support you today? Did you wonder about anything instead of trying to figure it out?
Quickly write down everything that comes to mind.

_____

_____

_____

_____

_____

_____

_____

_____

_____

_____

_____

_____

_____

_____

_____

_____

Take a few deep breaths and relax.

INTUITIVE MESSAGE
Wonder.

DAY

6

Being playful frees both your creative and intuitive minds. Einstein called *play* the best form of research. Your barking dog/ego is not playful. It is too fearful, defensive, and insecure to let go and have fun. Your spirit, on the other hand, is full of humor, spontaneity, and playfulness. The more playful you are, the more inspiration and intuition flows.

MORNING JOURNALING:

How does your spirit enjoy playing? When was the last time you engaged in a playful experience? What makes your spirit laugh? Did you have any time to play today?

_____

_____

_____

_____

_____

_____

_____

_____

Playing opens the door to great inspiration and inner guidance.

EVENING REFLECTION:

What makes your spirit come alive? Did you do anything playful
today? Did your barking dog/ego ruin the fun?
Quickly write down everything that comes to mind.

_____

_____

_____

_____

_____

_____

_____

_____

_____

_____

_____

_____

_____

_____

_____

Take a few deep breaths and relax.

INTUITIVE MESSAGE
Be playful.

7

MORNING JOURNALING:

Did you meditate this week? Create your room to breathe? Drink enough water?

_____

_____

_____

_____

Did you wonder instead of worry?

_____

_____

_____

What was the most valuable thing you learned or discovered about yourself this week?

_____

_____

_____

_____

What was the most playful thing you did this week?

_____

_____

_____

_____

What was your biggest intuitive "aha"?

_____

_____

_____

_____

_____

What are you most grateful for this week?

_____

_____

_____

_____

_____

_____

What have you *happily* let go of?

INTUITIVE MESSAGE
Always trust your vibes.

WEEK 9 This week you will focus on developing confidence in your intuition.

DAY

1

Intuition and ego have very different vibrations. Intuition, the channel of your heart, is calm, consistent, and direct. It communicates with few or no words at all, just a feeling. Your barking dog/ego, on the other hand, the channel in your head, is noisy, inconsistent, talks too much, and flip-flops. The heart brings reassurance, serenity, and comfort. The head brings anxiety, chaos, and conflict. One leaves you feeling good, and the other leaves you feeling threatened. Recognize the difference.

MORNING JOURNALING:

Consciously recognizing the energetic difference between your barking dog/ego and your intuitive spirit will keep you from confusing the two.
What is your greatest challenge today?

_____

_____

_____

_____

Now invite both your barking dog/ego and your intuitive spirit to offer you guidance.
Fill in the blank: My barking dog says _____.

Continue writing until it has nothing more to say.

_____

_____

_____

Take a deep breath. Exhale with a loud sigh, and shift your attention to your heart.
Then, fill in the following: My spirit says _____.
Again, write until there's nothing more to say.

_____

_____

_____

Feel the energetic difference between what your barking dog/ego says and what your spirit says. Then listen to what *feels true*.

EVENING REFLECTION:

Who did you listen to? Your barking dog/ego or your spirit? What was the best thing that happened today? Quickly write down everything that comes to mind.

_____

_____

_____

_____

Take a few deep breathes and relax.

INTUITIVE MESSAGE
Tune in to the heart.

DAY

2

Don't let the negativity of your own barking dog/ego or the pessimism of others convince you that what you seek, desire, or want to create isn't possible. Not only are all things possible, but following your vibes will quickly guide you directly to your heart's desire if you don't allow anything to interfere.

MORNING JOURNALING:

What would you love to experience or attract more than anything right now? Do you believe it is possible? What guidance do your vibes offer toward successfully achieving this? Has anyone tried to interfere with this or discourage you from believing in yourself? Is your barking dog/ego discouraging you or keeping you from believing in yourself?

_____

_____

_____

_____

_____

_____

Listen to your heart today, not your barking dog/ego, or others' barking dogs/egos. Keep your dreams private so others won't try to steal them away.

EVENING REFLECTION:

How did your vibes move you toward your dreams today? Did anyone's barking dog/ego, including your own, get in the way? What was the best thing that happened today?
Quickly write down everything that comes to mind.

_____

_____

_____

_____

_____

_____

_____

_____

_____

_____

_____

_____

_____

_____

_____

_____

Take a few deep breaths and relax.

INTUITIVE MESSAGE
Go for it!

DAY

3

We often don't trust our vibes because others have told us, or they've implied, that we can't trust ourselves. Authority figures and controlling others discourage us, for one reason or another, from having faith in ourselves, or confidence in our intuitive ability to lead our lives. They are wrong.

MORNING JOURNALING:

Has anyone in your past discouraged you or implied that you cannot trust yourself or your inner guidance? Has anyone deterred you from trusting your vibes lately? Is there anyone trying to control you or take away your autonomy or right to direct your life the way you want?

_____

_____

_____

_____

_____

_____

_____

_____

Believe in your spirit. Your spirit can take care of you. Be your own best champion and cheerleader, and trust your vibes today, even if others try to interfere or try to make you doubt yourself.

EVENING REFLECTION:

What did you notice today that you hadn't before? How did your intuition support you today? What was the best part of your day? Quickly write down everything that comes to mind.

_____

_____

_____

_____

_____

_____

_____

_____

_____

_____

_____

_____

_____

_____

_____

Take a few deep breaths and relax.

INTUITIVE MESSAGE
Be your own authority.

DAY
4

MORNING VIBE CHECK:

Today we will vibe check the immediate path ahead.

To begin, take a deep breath through the nose, and then exhale, as if you're blowing out candles, and with it, completely empty everything you are holding on to or that is holding on to you. Repeat this a few times or until your mind feels empty and quiet.

Once you complete this step, close your eyes, turn your attention inward, and enter your imagination. Imagine a big screen lights up at a 45-degree angle above your eyes. Project the immediate future onto the screen. Slowly scan the path ahead, starting with the present moment, and clairvoyantly look ahead to the next month or two. As you scan, see if you intuitively sense any changes or shifts. Don't intellectualize or overthink. Let your imagination go wild, and be curious without attachment about what you sense or intuitively see. Simply notice everything that spontaneously comes to mind.

When you sense something, stop, and ask the following questions:

"What is unfolding?" "What is important to know?" "What will I attract or encounter in the next three months?"

Answer quickly with the first thing that enters your mind. Don't try to be logical or justify what you feel, because you won't be able to. Just trust what spontaneously shows up, knowing your vibes work best this way.

Your vibe check revealed:

_____

_____

_____

_____

_____

_____

When you have finished, set it aside. Revisit your responses later in the day. Vibe checks reveal probabilities, or, in other words, reflect the way the energy is lined up but not yet set in stone. Like a GPS, your vibes simply reflect the road ahead from an immediate vantage point. Life, like moving traffic, has patterns but can unexpectedly change. Having a general intuitive sense of things to come can help you make better decisions today.

EVENING REFLECTION:

What did you discover when vibe checking today? What did your path ahead reveal?
Quickly write your response.

_____

_____

_____

_____

_____

_____

When you are finished writing, fully relax.

INTUITIVE MESSAGE
Vibe check everything and often.

5

Following the light of your spirit is the most empowering and healing choice you can make because it keeps you in alignment with who you really are, sets clear boundaries, alerts you to danger, directs you to opportunity, and keeps you faithful to what is in your best interest and away from what is not. Nothing and no one else can do a better job for you on keeping you healthy, happy, and whole.

MORNING JOURNALING:

How has your inner guidance ever helped you so far? Do you feel more connected to your authentic Self? Are you any more aligned with your spirit? Are your insides and outsides starting to match up?

_____

_____

_____

_____

_____

_____

_____

_____

_____

Trusting your vibes keeps you real.

EVENING REFLECTION:

What did your vibes notice today that you hadn't before? How did your intuition help you today? What did you learn today? Quickly write down everything that comes to mind.

_____

_____

_____

_____

_____

_____

_____

_____

_____

_____

_____

_____

_____

_____

_____

_____

Take a few deep breaths and relax.

INTUITIVE MESSAGE
Follow the light.

DAY

6

Every day, you face the need to make choices. You can choose to stay true to yourself, be in your heart, and trust and act on your vibes. Doing this allows you to live in an authentic and empowered way. Or you can choose to listen to your barking dog/ego, let others overwhelm and control you, and feel disappointed and victimized after the fact, and lead a disempowered life. You decide.

MORNING JOURNALING:

What choices are you making today?

_____

_____

_____

_____

_____

_____

_____

_____

_____

_____

Choose to follow your spirit today.

EVENING REFLECTION:

What are your top priorities today? Did you listen to your spirit or
your barking dog/ego? Are you happy with the choices you made?
Quickly write down everything that comes to mind.

_____

_____

_____

_____

_____

_____

_____

_____

_____

_____

_____

_____

_____

_____

_____

_____

Take a few deep breaths and relax.

INTUITIVE MESSAGE
Choose your authentic self.

7

MORNING JOURNALING:

Did you meditate this week? Drink water? Slow down? Breathe?

_____

_____

_____

_____

What are you most grateful for this week?

_____

_____

_____

_____

What was the most valuable thing you learned or discovered about yourself this week?

_____

_____

_____

_____

What was the biggest obstacle to trusting your vibes?

_____

_____

_____

Did you follow the light of your spirit or the noise of your barking dog/ego?

_____

_____

Are you feeling more congruent and in integrity these days?

_____

_____

_____

What was the biggest blessing you received this week?

_____

_____

_____

How well are you feeling lately?

_____

_____

_____

INTUITIVE MESSAGE
Always trust your vibes.

WEEK 10

This week you will focus on removing hidden obstacles to your inner guidance.

DAY

1

Meditating daily is the foundation of an intuitively guided life. It trains your mind to be more observant, less reactive to the circumstances around you, and more attuned to the guiding spirit within. It lowers your stress and increases your vitality. It's like going to an inner spa and refreshing yourself every morning. Don't leave home without it.

MORNING JOURNALING:

Have you been regularly meditating? How has your life changed since you started meditating? What is getting in the way if you aren't meditating regularly?

_____

_____

_____

_____

_____

_____

Reflect on the power that meditation offers. Take that power into your day.

EVENING REFLECTION:

How has meditating regularly helped you? If you aren't meditating, how noisy is your barking dog/ego? Are you tired of it? Quickly write down everything that comes to mind.

_____

_____

_____

_____

_____

_____

_____

_____

_____

_____

_____

_____

_____

_____

_____

_____

Take a few deep breaths and relax.

INTUITIVE MESSAGE
Continue to meditate.

DAY

2

Your barking dog/ego, when untrained, attacks your spirit through relentless self-criticism and the sinking feeling of never being good enough. Listening to the self-criticism and self-denigration of your barking dog/ego wounds you deeply. Train your barking dog/ego, with meditation and movement, to be quiet. Stop allowing these attacks on your spirit. Be intolerant of an unruly barking dog/ego that causes pain and chaos in your life.

MORNING JOURNALING:

In what way do you criticize yourself? Do you compare yourself unfavorably with others? Do you criticize your body? Your level of achievement? Something else? Answer quickly, and then, in place of criticism, give yourself three genuine and earned compliments. What do you love and appreciate most about yourself?

Read aloud what you've written. Then, today, go on a self-criticism fast. When you accidentally criticize yourself or put yourself down in any way, the minute you realize it, say, "Stop!" out loud, followed by "I love myself." It will reconnect you with your spirit and stop this self-attack.

EVENING REFLECTION:

Name three things you did or said today that you love, are proud of, and make you feel good about yourself. More if you can think of more. Quickly write down the response.

1 _____

_____

_____

2 _____

_____

_____

3 _____

_____

_____

When you finish, take a few deep breaths. Recognize the magnificent spirit within you, and smile. What's not to love?

INTUITIVE MESSAGE
Love yourself unconditionally.

DAY

3

All humans make mistakes. While we can't avoid this, we can learn from these mistakes. Forgive your mistakes once you learn the lessons they bring, so you are available to what is happening now. Receive the gifts of your experience, forgive yourself, and move on.

MORNING JOURNALING:

Are there things you regret, feel ashamed of, are embarrassed by, or hide, that interfere with your confidence and self-love today? What have you learned from these experiences? What are you now ready to forgive so you can be fully present? This is energetic garbage, and it's time to empty it.

Read aloud what you've written. Forgive as much as possible today. It isn't worth it to carry it any farther.

EVENING REFLECTION:

What was the best part of your day? Where and with whom did your spirit shine through? In what way were you most present? What are you willing to forgive and let go of?
Quickly write down the response.

_____

_____

_____

_____

_____

_____

_____

_____

_____

_____

_____

When you finish, take a few deep breaths. The more energetic garbage from the past we empty through forgiveness, the more peaceful our day and sleep become.

INTUITIVE MESSAGE
Empty the garbage.

DAY

4

MORNING VIBE CHECK:

Today we will vibe check your body to release the past.

To begin, take a deep breath through the nose, and then exhale, as if you're blowing out candles, and with it, completely empty everything you are holding on to or that is holding on to you. Repeat this a few times or until your mind feels empty and quiet.

Once you complete this step, close your eyes, turn your attention inward, and enter your imagination. Slowly scan your body. Starting with the feet and moving up to the crown, scan for any energy leftover from the past that is asking to be accepted and released now. Don't intellectualize or overthink. Simply notice everything you spontaneously sense or feel, however subtle, and trust what comes to mind.

When you sense something, stop, and ask the following questions:

"Who is this?" "What is this about?" "What wants to be released now?"

Answer quickly with the first thing that enters your mind, knowing your body tells the truth.

Your vibe check revealed:

_____

_____

_____

_____

_____

_____

When you have finished, set it aside, take a deep breath, and exhale, and with it, sweep through your body and imagine everything holding on from the past is now being released. Breathe in fresh air for a new day, freed from the past.

EVENING REFLECTION:

What did you forgive in yourself? What was the best experience of the day? How did your vibes help?
Quickly write your response.

_____

_____

_____

_____

_____

_____

_____

_____

_____

_____

_____

_____

When you are finished writing, fully relax. Breathe in. Accept. Exhale. Let go.

INTUITIVE MESSAGE
Vibe check everything and often.

DAY

5

When you forgive those who've hurt you, you return to your spirit, and healing begins. You cut the cords to the past, free up your awareness, reconnect to your intuition and power, and regain the ability to create something new.

MORNING JOURNALING:

Who or what in your life do you need to forgive? Who or what in your life is tough to forgive, but you'd like to? Who or what in your life is it extremely difficult to forgive and you're not ready to yet?

_____

_____

_____

_____

_____

_____

_____

_____

Read aloud what you've written. To forgive is a hugely empowering and healing decision. Often grief and wounding need time and space to heal before forgiveness becomes possible. Take your time, but consider forgiving a little bit more today.

EVENING REFLECTION:

Who did you forgive today? A bad driver? A slow waiter? A mistake a co-worker made? Your mother? Every choice to forgive counts. A little forgiveness eventually leads to more because it feels so good. Quickly write down the response.

_____

_____

_____

_____

_____

_____

_____

_____

_____

_____

_____

_____

When you finish, take a few deep breaths. The more you forgive, the more your inner light flows through your heart, and the more peaceful and guided you become.

INTUITIVE MESSAGE
Forgive at your own pace.

DAY

6

Comparing yourself to others is a toxic mistake. No matter how it adds up, comparison will never leave you feeling good about yourself. Either you'll feel superior, which leaves you isolated and stressed to maintain your position, or you'll feel insecure because there will always be someone who can threaten your position. Or you will feel inferior, which leaves you feeling anxious, resentful, insecure, and angry. Comparing yourself to others negates your self-worth and leaves you feeling you are never good enough. This merry-go-round deteriorates your well-being and erodes your confidence and inner peace every time. It is a lose-lose toxic temptation that attacks your well-being, and you are advised to avoid it at all costs.

MORNING JOURNALING:

Who are you tempted to compare yourself with right now? Have you felt others comparing themselves to you? How has that left you feeling? How has comparison taken away your joy and self-esteem?

_____

_____

_____

_____

_____

_____

Read aloud what you've written.

EVENING REFLECTION:

Did you fall into the trap of comparing yourself with anyone today? Were you aware of anyone comparing themself with you? What was the best thing that happened to you today? In what way did your spirit shine through?
Quickly write down the response.

_____

_____

_____

_____

_____

_____

_____

_____

_____

_____

_____

_____

_____

_____

When you finish, take a few deep breaths.

INTUITIVE MESSAGE
Never compare.

MORNING JOURNALING:

Did you meditate this week? Drink water? Remember to breathe?
Eat healthy food?

_____

_____

_____

_____

_____

_____

Who and what did you love most this week?

_____

_____

_____

_____

_____

_____

_____

What was the most valuable thing you learned or discovered about yourself this week?

_____

_____

_____

_____

_____

What did you forgive and are now willing to release?

_____

_____

_____

_____

What was the best gift you received this week?

_____

_____

_____

_____

_____

_____

INTUITIVE MESSAGE
Always trust your vibes.

DAY

1

Your inner guidance leads you to the most congruent, harmonious life possible—one where your head, heart, gut, and feet are aligned with your spirit and moving in the direction of your highest good. Physically you will feel at ease. Mentally you will feel clear and confident. Emotionally you will feel calm, present, and available. Spiritually you will feel connected to your Divine Self and the loving Universe. Overall, you will feel grounded and peaceful. The key to such congruency is to be honest with yourself, listen to your heart, and courageously trust your vibes.

MORNING JOURNALING:

What do you honestly want most in your life right now? Are you hiding anything from yourself? From others? Do you feel in alignment with your spirit?

_____

_____

_____

_____

_____

Is there any part of you that feels out of alignment with your spirit? Today, be congruent.

EVENING REFLECTION:

Which intention did you focus on today? How did your inner guidance help? What was the best part of the day?
Quickly write down your response.

_____

_____

_____

_____

_____

_____

_____

_____

_____

_____

_____

_____

_____

_____

_____

_____

When you finish, take a few deep breaths and relax. You deserve it.

INTUITIVE MESSAGE
Live congruently.

DAY

2

Toxic energy is harmful to your spirit. It destabilizes your inner guidance and overwhelms your nervous system. If around it long enough, toxic energy can even make you sick. Toxic energy comes from addiction, anger, aggression, low self-esteem, blame, victimhood, rage, criticism, jealousy, manipulation, judgment, and attack, from self and others. If you want to live an intuitively guided, spiritually congruent, empowered life, recognize, and remove yourself from toxicity, inside and out.

MORNING JOURNALING:

Are you around anyone whose energy feels toxic to you? Are you toxic to yourself? Do you regularly interact with toxic people or just occasionally? Can you manage how frequently you are exposed to this toxic energy? Or do you feel you have no choice? Are you creating toxic energy yourself? Do you have addictions or emotional challenges that need to be addressed now? Are you ready to clear toxic energy from your life? You don't have to do it alone, but you do have to be willing to do it.

Read aloud what you wrote. You have a choice when it comes to being around toxic energy. Even though it may be uncomfortable to make a self-loving choice, disengaging from toxic energy as fast as you can is the sanest, most self-loving choice.

EVENING REFLECTION:

Did you experience toxic energy today? Were you able to lovingly walk away? If yes, congratulations. If not, love yourself anyway. This may be a new option to consider and may take some awareness and practice. Don't worry. You'll catch on.
Quickly write down your response.

_____

_____

_____

_____

_____

_____

_____

_____

_____

_____

When you finish, take a few deep breaths.

INTUITIVE MESSAGE
If it's toxic, remove yourself.

DAY

3

It's hard to get a clear, intuitive read on something or someone if strong emotions are scrambling your intuitive channels. To clear an emotional storm, acknowledge your strong emotions, including resentment, anger, bitterness, fear, jealousy, judgment, or more. Then exhale these vibrations as if you are emptying the garbage. Do this as many times as necessary to feel peaceful and clear. It's no use trying to tap into intuitive guidance when you are swirling in clouds of emotional reactivity or feeling emotionally triggered in some way.

MORNING JOURNALING:

Is there any area of your life, or any one person or people whose negative emotions make it difficult for you to tune in to your intuition? Do you harbor fear, anger, jealousy, or resentment toward anyone, past or present, for example? Are you struggling at work or with in-laws, neighbors, partners, anyone? Are you suffering from chronic emotional upset, such as PTSD?

_____

_____

_____

_____

_____

When you acknowledge negative or hurt feelings, you bring them into the open, where they can begin to move on. Once this starts to happen, your intuitive channels begin working again.

EVENING REFLECTION:

Did you release any intense emotions today? What was the best part of your day? How did your intuition help?
Quickly write down your response.

When you finish, take a few deep breaths. And a few more. This helps release old, stuck, negative emotions and opens your intuitive channels once again, so you can heal.

INTUITIVE MESSAGE
Let the storms pass.

DAY

4

MORNING VIBE CHECK:

Today you are going to vibe check your health.

To begin, take a deep breath through the nose, and then exhale, as if you're blowing out candles, and with it, completely empty everything you are holding on to or that is holding on to you. Repeat this a few times or until your mind feels empty and quiet.

Once you complete this step, close your eyes, turn your attention inward, and slowly scan your body, starting at the feet and moving up to your crown. As you scan each area of your body, notice or sense any subtle energy that is holding on, trying to get your attention. Pay special attention to any area of the body that feels painful, weak, tense, tight, or simply doesn't feel "right." Don't intellectualize or overthink. Simply notice everything you spontaneously sense or feel, however subtle, and trust that by focusing on it your intuition can communicate important information about your experience right now.

When you sense something, stop, and ask the following questions:

"What is this energy about?" "What can I learn from this?" "Who is this energy concerning?" "What would this energy like me to know?"

Answer quickly with the first thing that enters your mind. Don't try to be logical or justify what you feel, because you won't be able to. Trust what spontaneously comes to mind, knowing your inner guidance is subtly communicating important information that will keep you safe, protected, and moving in the direction of your highest good through the energy you are sensing. This is how your intuition works. Don't fight it. Lean into it. If you do, it will work for you.

Your vibe check revealed:

_____

_____

_____

_____

_____

_____

Stop and occasionally vibe check as you move through your day.

EVENING REFLECTION:

What did your body vibe check advise on your health? Are you ignoring any vibes concerning your physical well-being? What was the happiest part of your day?
Quickly write down everything that comes to mind.

_____

_____

_____

_____

_____

_____

_____

Take a few deep breaths and relax.

INTUITIVE MESSAGE
Vibe check for health.

5

Rather than wasting time asking your limited barking dog/ego to figure things out in your life, simply ask your all-knowing spirit for guidance instead. Then drink a glass of water, breathe deeply, exhale everything you're holding on to, and listen to your heart.

MORNING JOURNALING:

Write down three pressing questions that you'd like to ask your intuition.

1 _____

2 _____

3 _____

Now ask your spirit for guidance on each concern, and write the response below.

1 _____

2 _____

3 _____

Read aloud what you wrote. Can you feel whether the responses came from your spirit or your barking dog/ego, trying to pose as your spirit? Were the answers short and to the point? If yes, then it's your spirit. If they were rambling, confusing, and led you in circles, then it's your barking dog/ego.

EVENING REFLECTION:

Write down a burning question that you want to ask your spirit now. Ask your spirit to give you the answer while you sleep. Quickly write down your question.

_____

_____

_____

_____

_____

_____

_____

_____

_____

_____

_____

_____

_____

_____

When you finish, take a few deep breaths. Relax. Your spirit is on the job.

INTUITIVE MESSAGE
Go directly to your source.

6

Trusting your vibes is a powerful decision. When you make that decision, you embrace your authentic Self and allow your spirit to take care of you instead of placing your well-being in the hands of those who can't possibly do a good job.

MORNING JOURNALING:

Write down three questions you need answers to now.

1 _____

2 _____

3 _____

Now let your spirit answer each question.

1 _____

2 _____

3 _____

Read aloud what you wrote. Do the answers leave you feeling secure and reassured? If yes, it's your intuition. If not, ask again later.

EVENING REFLECTION:

What was the most helpful guidance you received today from your spirit? What was the best thing that happened today? Quickly write down your response.

_____

When you finish, take a few deep breaths.

INTUITIVE MESSAGE
Ask your spirit instead of others.

MORNING JOURNALING:

Ask your spirit for guidance, and then quickly write down what you receive.

_____

_____

_____

_____

_____

How have you steered clear of toxicity? With whom?

_____

_____

_____

_____

What was the most valuable thing you learned or discovered about yourself this week?

_____

_____

_____

_____

What was the biggest gift this week?

_____

_____

_____

_____

What was your greatest intuitive insight?

_____

_____

_____

_____

What are you most grateful for this week?

_____

_____

_____

What have you *happily let go of*?

_____

_____

_____

_____

_____

INTUITIVE MESSAGE
Always trust your vibes.

WEEK 12

This week you will focus on attracting support.

DAY

1

If you cannot resolve an issue no matter how hard you try, then turn the situation over to your spirit and sleep on it for two nights in a row. Ask your spirit to reveal the solution while you sleep. Be open to receiving an answer during this time.

MORNING JOURNALING:

What issues are you struggling with right now? Where do you feel stuck? Where would you like guidance but haven't been successful so far in receiving it? What do you feel is blocking you from getting guidance?

_____

_____

_____

_____

_____

_____

Read aloud what you wrote. Let it go for the next two days, and then check in with your intuition again.

If you say you want guidance but can't seem to get any, perhaps it's because you're secretly blocking it. Do you feel that you are blocking guidance in any area of your life? If the answer is yes, then why are you blocking it? What are you afraid of?
Quickly write down your response.

_____

_____

_____

_____

_____

_____

_____

_____

_____

_____

_____

_____

_____

When you finish, take a few deep breaths. Give everything a break.

INTUITIVE MESSAGE
Sleep on it.

DAY

2

The more grateful you are, the more your heart opens, the higher your vibration elevates, and the more intuitively guided you will be. The more "green lights" you meet, the more your heart's desires are fulfilled.

MORNING JOURNALING:

List the top 10 things that you are grateful for today.

1 _____

2 _____

3 _____

4 _____

5 _____

6 _____

7 _____

8 _____

9 _____

10 _____

Read aloud what you wrote. Notice how healing and encouraging to your mind, body, and spirit being grateful is. Gratitude is healing.

EVENING REFLECTION:

What was the most surprising gift you received today? Can you find anything to be grateful for in the most difficult aspects of your life? Quickly write down your response.

_____

_____

_____

_____

_____

_____

_____

_____

_____

_____

_____

_____

_____

_____

_____

When you finish, take a few deep breaths. The more grateful you are, the more secure, confident calm, and okay you will be.

INTUITIVE MESSAGE
Be grateful for everything.

3

One of our greatest fears in life is not belonging. Humans have a primal fear of being rejected and left alone. This plays a big role in why so many people ignore their intuition. They fear rejection and lack the support they need to follow their inner guidance openly and happily. We need kindred spirits, people who believe in us and encourage us to trust our heart and spirit to overcome this primal fear. These people are members of what is known as your "soul family." They do exist, and it is up to us to recognize them.

MORNING JOURNALING:

List three people who leave you feeling as though you fully belong and welcome your presence—three people you recognize as soul family members.

1 _____

2 _____

3 _____

Today, tell your soul family how important they are to you and how much they have helped you live in an authentic and empowering way.

EVENING REFLECTION:

Did you deeply connect with anyone in your family of origin today? Have you met anyone else you deeply connect with? Can you identify your soul family members? Sometimes you don't have to even speak to soul family members directly to feel connected; simply thinking of them opens your heart. You always feel deeply loved, accepted, and connected. Quickly write down the names of your soul family members.

_____

_____

_____

_____

_____

_____

_____

_____

_____

_____

_____

_____

_____

_____

_____

When you finish, take a few deep breaths and relax. You are aligning with your true Self more and more each day.

INTUITIVE MESSAGE
Find your people.

DAY

4

MORNING VIBE CHECK:

Today you will vibe check anything you want. First, review the basic vibe check steps, and then focus your attention on what it is you're specifically interested in vibe checking.

To begin, take a deep breath through the nose, and then exhale, as if you're blowing out candles, and with it, completely empty everything you are holding on to or that is holding on to you. Repeat this a few times or until your mind feels empty and quiet.

Once you complete this step, close your eyes, turn your attention inward, and slowly scan your area of interest or concern. Be organized as you scan. For example, if scanning a person, scan their body, feet to crown. If scanning an event, scan the duration or location of the event. If scanning a potential business decision, scan all people involved. As you scan your concern, notice all subtle energy that calls to your attention. Pay special attention to any energy that feels off-balance, ungrounded, unsafe, misaligned with you, or simply doesn't feel right. Also notice if there is anything about your area of concern that feels particularly positive, warm, connected, uplifting, attractive, fortunate, and appealing. In other words, is this area of concern a positive vibrational match with you? Don't intellectualize or overthink. Simply notice everything you spontaneously sense or feel, however subtle, and trust what comes to mind.

When you sense something, stop, and ask the following questions:

"What is this energy about?" "What can I learn from this?" "How can I correct this?" (if you sense a problem), or "How can I take advantage of this?" (if you sense an opportunity).

Answer quickly with the first thing that enters your mind. Don't try to be logical or justify what you feel, because you won't be

able to. Trust what spontaneously comes to mind, knowing your intuition works perfectly through this method if you relax into it.

Your vibe check revealed:

_____

_____

_____

_____

_____

Stop and occasionally vibe check as you move through your day.

EVENING REFLECTION:

What did your body vibe check advise on your area of concern or interest? Was this a surprise or had you been intuitively feeling it already? What was the happiest part of your day?

Quickly write down everything that comes to mind.

_____

_____

_____

_____

_____

Take a few deep breaths and relax.

INTUITIVE MESSAGE
Vibe check everything and often.

DAY

5

Maya Angelou is quoted as saying, "When people show you who they are, believe them." Pay attention to the actions and behaviors of the people in your life. Are these actions and behaviors congruent with your values and priorities? Are you around negative people who tend to sabotage your well-being? Are you wasting time trying to change these people? Are you in denial that they are having such a negative impact on you? Are you over-giving to these people, hoping your generosity will kick-start their own, to no avail? Be honest about the company you keep. If you're in bad company, move on.

MORNING JOURNALING:

Do you know negative people who tend to bring you down? Are you around people who tend to look on the worst side of life? This can be in person or on the news or radio. Have you noticed how listening to all this negative input shuts off your intuitive channels and can demoralize your spirit? What do you listen to in a day, and how does it affect you?

_____

_____

_____

_____

_____

_____

The more aware and discerning you are about what you listen to, the easier it is to raise your own consciousness so that you can receive guidance from your spirit.

The barking dog/ego noise and your head say _____.

_____

_____

_____

_____

EVENING REFLECTION:

Were you able to walk away from barking dog/ego noise today? What was the most uplifting, reassuring, intuitive experience you had today?

_____

_____

_____

_____

_____

_____

_____

_____

When you are done relaxing, enjoy the quiet in your head.

INTUITIVE MESSAGE
Be discerning.

DAY

6

The barking dog/ego mind dwells on the problems of life and often gets backed into a corner, feeling there's no way out. The intuitive spirit, on the other hand, dwells on solutions, and sees many creative ways forward. Brainstorming to discover solutions to problems is a tremendously creative, fun way to activate your intuition at the highest level.

MORNING JOURNALING:

Write down your present greatest challenge, concern, or quandary. Next, invite your creative, intuitive spirit to come up with 19 possible solutions to this situation as quickly as possible. Be as creative or silly as you'd like to be when brainstorming answers. This effort activates the creative aspect of intuition, bringing new ideas, mind-blowing innovations, and surprising and workable solutions.

1 _____

2 _____

3 _____

4 _____

5 _____

6 _____

7 _____

8 _____

9 _____

10 _____

11 _____

12 _____

13 _____

14 _____

15 _____

16 _____

17 _____

18 _____

19 _____

Continue to brainstorm all day, knowing there is always a solution when you ask your intuition.

EVENING REFLECTION:

What did you notice today that you hadn't before? How did your intuition support you today? What was the best part of your day? Quickly write down everything that comes to mind.

_____

_____

_____

_____

Take a few deep breaths and relax.

INTUITIVE MESSAGE
There's always a solution.

MORNING JOURNALING:

Did you meditate this week? Drink water? Remember to breathe? Eat well?

_____

_____

_____

_____

_____

Did you do any brainstorming?

_____

_____

_____

_____

What was the most valuable thing you learned or discovered about yourself this week?

_____

_____

_____

_____

What was the biggest obstacle to trusting your vibes?

_____

_____

_____

_____

What are you most grateful for this week?

_____

_____

_____

_____

What was the biggest surprise of the week?

_____

_____

_____

_____

What were the biggest blessings you received this week?

_____

_____

_____

_____

INTUITIVE MESSAGE
Always trust your vibes.

DAY

1

If you want intuitive guidance but it isn't forthcoming, rather than continuing to struggle, trying to mentally figure how to best move ahead, go for a long walk instead. Walking is a powerful meditative practice that quiets the mind and opens the door to intuitive guidance. It will clear your head, ground you, and expel accumulated negative or overloaded energy in your field in the same way that a rainstorm clears the atmosphere. After a long walk, intuitive answers flow once again.

MORNING JOURNALING:

Have you ever solved a problem after you've gone for a long walk? Have you ever been inspired, received new ideas, or felt intuitive direction during or shortly after walking? Are you physically able to go for long walks?

_____

_____

_____

_____

_____

Make time to add a walk of any length into your weekly routine.

EVENING REFLECTION:

Were you able to take a walk today? If so, did you receive any clarity while you were walking? Afterward? How did your intuition support you today? What was the best part of your day? Quickly write down everything that comes to mind.

_____

_____

_____

_____

_____

_____

_____

_____

_____

_____

_____

_____

_____

_____

When you are finished, relax.

INTUITIVE MESSAGE
Walk on it.

DAY

2

An effective way to distinguish your ego from intuition is to voice your intuitive feelings out loud. Intuitive feelings originate in the heart and when spoken aloud have a warm, grounded, reassuring, resonance and tone. If your words come from your barking dog/ego, they feel energetically tinny, cool, brittle, and ungrounded, as if rolling around in your head like a metal ball in a pinball machine, never quite landing in a satisfactory, reassuring way.

MORNING JOURNALING:

Write down your top three pressing questions.

1 _____

2 _____

3 _____

Ask your spirit for guidance, and then quickly write down your answers.

1 _____

2 _____

3 _____

When you are done writing, read aloud what you've written. Notice the tone and feel of your words and where they originate in your body, head, or heart. If your words came from the heart, follow the guidance. If what you wrote came from your head, ignore it, and ask again later today—but next time answer out loud instead of writing it down.

EVENING REFLECTION:

Did you ask your spirit for guidance today? Did you answer out loud? Could you feel the guidance coming from your heart, or was it rolling around in your head?
Quickly write down your response.

When you finish, take a few deep breaths and relax.

INTUITIVE MESSAGE
Listen for the truth.

DAY

3

Intuition will guide you if you are genuinely available to receiving answers. Often when asking for intuitive guidance, unless you are genuinely open to guidance or available to hearing what might disappoint your ego, your intuition cannot get in. Therefore, only ask questions if you are receptive to receiving the whole truth, even if it might not be what you want to hear.

MORNING JOURNALING:

Do you have a question or concern but are afraid to ask, for fear of disappointment in the answer?
Write it down here.

_____

_____

_____

_____

What are you afraid of hearing?

_____

_____

_____

Now read your answers aloud. If your fear is unfounded, it will ease once out in the open. If what you wrote has merit and you deny it, you'll know this in your heart. Denial is no protection.

EVENING REFLECTION:

Were you genuinely available to intuitive guidance today? Were you open to receiving the truth so you could make the best decisions?
Quickly write down your response.

_____

_____

_____

_____

_____

_____

_____

_____

_____

_____

_____

_____

_____

_____

When you finish, take a few deep breaths and listen.

INTUITIVE MESSAGE
Be receptive.

DAY

4

MORNING VIBE CHECK:

Today, vibe check anything you want. First, review the basic vibe check steps, and then focus your attention on what it is you're specifically interested in vibe checking.

To begin, take a deep breath through the nose, and then exhale, as if you're blowing out candles, and with it, completely empty everything you are holding on to or that is holding on to you. Repeat this a few times or until your mind feels empty and quiet.

Once you complete this step, close your eyes, turn your attention inward, and slowly scan your area of interest or concern. Be organized as you go. For example, if scanning a person, scan their body, feet to crown. If scanning an event, scan the duration or location of the event. If scanning a potential business decision, scan all people involved. As you scan your concern, notice all subtle energy that calls to your attention. Pay special attention to any energy that feels off-balance, ungrounded, unsafe, misaligned with you, or simply doesn't feel right. Also notice if there is anything about your area of concern that feels particularly positive, warm, connected, uplifting, attractive, fortunate, and appealing. In other words, is this area of concern a positive vibrational match with you? Don't intellectualize or overthink. Simply notice everything you spontaneously sense or feel, however subtle, and trust what comes to mind.

When you sense something, stop, and ask the following questions:

"What is this energy about?" "What can I learn from this?" "How can I correct this?" (if you sense a problem), or "How can I take advantage of this?" (if you sense an opportunity).

Answer quickly with the first thing that enters your mind. Don't try to be logical or justify what you feel, because you won't be

able to. Trust what spontaneously comes to mind, knowing your intuition works perfectly through this method if you relax into it.

Your vibe check revealed:

_____

_____

_____

_____

_____

Stop and occasionally vibe check as you move through your day.

EVENING REFLECTION:

What did your body vibe check advise on your area of concern or interest? Was this a surprise or had you been intuitively feeling it already? What was the happiest part of your day?
Quickly write down everything that comes to mind.

_____

_____

_____

_____

_____

_____

Take a few deep breaths and relax.

INTUITIVE MESSAGE
Vibe check everything and often.

DAY

5

As children, many of us were trained to look to authority figures to make our decisions for us. Such conditioning set us up to believe that we needed their permission to move forward in life and implied, along with this, that we cannot trust ourselves. As an adult, this is no longer true. The power and permission to trust your vibes and follow your heart lie solely in your hands.

MORNING JOURNALING:

Do you tend to ask others for their input before making decisions? Are you discerning about whom you ask? Do you ask people whom you admire and trust for their input and guidance? Or are you nondiscriminatory and asking everyone for their input? Are you now turning your attention inward and asking your spirit for guidance instead?

_____

_____

_____

_____

_____

_____

_____

_____

EVENING REFLECTION:

Did you seek outside counsel today? If yes, from whom? Was it an authority figure? A colleague? A mentor? A partner or friend? Or just someone you know? Did you seek input from your spirit today? What was the best thing that happened today?
Quickly write down your response.

_____

_____

_____

_____

_____

_____

_____

_____

_____

_____

_____

_____

_____

_____

_____

_____

INTUITIVE MESSAGE
Keep it to yourself.

DAY

6

When you pay attention to your intuition, you shift and grow, evolving into an empowered person. This can be disruptive to people who perceive you otherwise. It's not uncommon that they will try to push you back into being the submissive, passive person they've known you to be in the past. Stand in your power and trust your vibes anyway.

MORNING JOURNALING:

Have you unsettled anyone with your newly empowered intuition coming to life? Have you noticed anyone close to you being critical or dismissive of you trusting your vibes? Is trusting your vibes disrupting your relationships? Are you willing to trust your vibes anyway, knowing they are simply asking your relationships to grow and evolve?

_____

_____

_____

_____

_____

_____

_____

_____

EVENING REFLECTION:

Are any of your relationships challenged because you are now listening to your vibes? Have your relationships improved since you've begun trusting your vibes more? How has your life improved this week because you trusted your vibes? What was the best thing that happened?
Quickly write down your response.

_____

_____

_____

_____

_____

_____

_____

_____

_____

_____

_____

_____

_____

When you finish, take a few deep breaths and exhale. Let your mind rest so you can hear your heart.

INTUITIVE MESSAGE
Don't let anyone hold you back.

7

MORNING JOURNALING:

What was the best way in which your intuition helped you this week?

_____

_____

_____

_____

What are you most grateful for this week?

_____

_____

_____

_____

What was the most valuable thing you learned or discovered about yourself this week?

_____

_____

_____

_____

_____

What was the biggest obstacle to trusting your vibes?

_____

_____

_____

How is trusting your vibes improving your life?

_____

_____

_____

Are you feeling more congruent and in integrity these days?

_____

_____

_____

What was the biggest blessing you received this week?

_____

_____

_____

What do you love most about trusting your vibes?

_____

_____

_____

INTUITIVE MESSAGE
Always trust your vibes.

WEEK 14 ∞

DAY

1

While certain routines are beneficial, such as meditating daily, going for a walk, and asking for help, other routines can numb you out, keep you stuck in a rut, and shut down your intuitive channels. The antidote to mind-numbing routines is to expand your world and have an adventure. Make it a habit to seek out new things. Explore a new neighborhood, try an ethnic restaurant, enjoy live entertainment, and travel to new places. These experiences capture your attention, make you present, pique your curiosity, and awaken your sixth sense. Get out of your rut and have a more adventurous life.

MORNING JOURNALING:

What is the most adventurous thing you've done in the past month? In the past year? What do you routinely do that you are willing to change for the sake of having an adventure and waking up your spirit?

_____

_____

_____

_____

Make plans for an adventure today. Do something different.

EVENING REFLECTION:

What new thing did you discover today? Make any plans to try
something new?

_____

_____

_____

_____

_____

_____

_____

_____

_____

_____

_____

_____

_____

When you finish writing, take a few deep breaths and exhale.
Then relax.

INTUITIVE MESSAGE
Change your routines.

DAY
2

Inner guidance originates in the heart, the home of your Divine Spirit. The more you live in your open heart, the more naturally intuitive and in flow you will be. Being kind to others brings you back to your heart and spiritual home. It's the gift that keeps on giving.

MORNING JOURNALING:

Is your reaction to others generally kind and open or suspicious and guarded? Do you find it easier to be kind to one type of person over another? Can you imagine being kind to someone who is unkind to you?

List all the benefits you can think of for being kind to others no matter how they treat you.

_____

_____

_____

_____

_____

_____

_____

_____

_____

EVENING REFLECTION:

Was anyone particularly kind to you today? If yes, how did that feel? Were you able to be consciously kind to others even when it was challenging? How did that feel? How did your intuition help you today?

_____

_____

_____

_____

_____

_____

_____

_____

_____

_____

_____

_____

_____

_____

When you finish, take a few deep breaths and exhale. Relax.

INTUITIVE MESSAGE
Be kind.

DAY

3

The Universe often assists you by sending you earth angels in the way of people who help you, support you, are kind and generous with you, and make your life a little easier. Some show up as advisors, others as helpers, some as support people, some as new friends, and some as kind strangers. Recognizing earth angels and thanking them for making your life better attracts even more earth angels, who will do more of the same.

MORNING JOURNALING:

Who are your primary earth angels? How do they help you, or how have they helped you? Did you acknowledge any of them today? Have you told any of your earth angels how much you love them lately?

_____

_____

_____

_____

_____

_____

_____

Directly acknowledge and thank your earth angels today.

EVENING REFLECTION:

Did you thank those who helped you today? If yes, how was your appreciation received? How did your intuition help you with this?

_____

_____

_____

_____

_____

_____

_____

_____

_____

_____

_____

_____

_____

_____

When you finish, take a few deep breaths and exhale. Pat yourself on the back, for you, too, are an earth angel.

INTUITIVE MESSAGE
Say, "Thank you."

DAY

4

MORNING VIBE CHECK:

Today, vibe check anything you want. First, review the basic vibe check steps, and then you can focus your attention on what it is you're specifically interested in vibe checking.

To begin, take a deep breath through the nose, and then exhale, as if you're blowing out candles, and with it, completely empty everything you are holding on to or that is holding on to you. Repeat this a few times or until your mind feels empty and quiet.

Once you complete this step, close your eyes, turn your attention inward, and slowly scan your area of interest or concern. Be organized. For example, if scanning a person, scan their body, feet to crown. If scanning an event, scan the duration or location of the event. If scanning a potential business decision, scan all people involved. As you scan your concern, notice all subtle energy that calls to your attention. Pay special attention to any energy that feels off-balance, ungrounded, unsafe, misaligned with you, or simply doesn't feel right. Also notice if there is anything about your area of concern that feels particularly positive, warm, connected, uplifting, attractive, fortunate, and appealing. In other words, is this area of concern a positive vibrational match with you? Don't intellectualize or overthink. Simply notice everything you spontaneously sense or feel, however subtle, and trust what comes to mind.

When you sense something, stop, and ask the following questions:

"What is this energy about?" "What can I learn from this?" "How can I correct this?" (if you sense a problem), or "How can I take advantage of this?"(if you sense an opportunity).

Answer quickly with the first thing that enters your mind. Don't try to be logical or justify what you feel, because you won't be

able to. Trust what spontaneously comes to mind, knowing your intuition works perfectly through this method if you relax into it.
Your vibe check revealed:

_____

_____

_____

_____

_____

Stop and occasionally vibe check as you move through your day.

EVENING REFLECTION:

What did your body vibe check advise on your area of concern or interest? Was this a surprise or had you been intuitively feeling it already? What was the happiest part of your day?
Quickly write down everything that comes to mind.

_____

_____

_____

_____

_____

_____

Take a few deep breaths and relax.

INTUITIVE MESSAGE
Vibe check everything and often.

DAY

5

Being intuitive is an art, not a science, because it comes from your spirit and not your ego or logical brain. One of the most effective ways to jump-start your intuition is to do something creative. Whether it's painting, taking photos, baking a cake, playing the piano or guitar, designing a new outfit, or rearranging your furniture, these activities take you out of your nonintuitive, logical ego brain and put you into your highly intuitive imagination. Being creative opens the front door to your spirit and lets your intuitive inspiration flow.

MORNING JOURNALING:

What creative things do you love? What creative things do you do regularly? What creative things do you do occasionally? What creative thing would you love to do but haven't tried yet?

_____

_____

_____

_____

_____

_____

_____

_____

Look over your list. Choose one thing on this list and do it today.

EVENING REFLECTION:

What creative thing did you do today? Did you receive any intuitive inspiration or downloads?

_____

_____

_____

_____

_____

_____

_____

_____

_____

_____

_____

_____

_____

When you finish, take a few deep breaths and exhale. Everything in life is a creation.

INTUITIVE MESSAGE
Create as a spiritual practice.

DAY

6

Our spirit recognizes that there is no "them"— there's just "us," as we are all Spirit. We don't need others' approval to belong. We are loved. We belong and always have.

MORNING JOURNALING:

Do you feel at ease and comfortable no matter who you're around? Or do you feel the need for approval and therefore find yourself on guard and insecure?

_____

_____

_____

_____

_____

_____

_____

_____

Review what you wrote. If you are at ease, your spirit is in charge. If you are seeking approval, your barking dog/ego is in charge. Who do you want to be in charge today?

EVENING REFLECTION:

Who oversees your life today? Your barking dog/ego or your beautiful spirit?

_____

_____

_____

_____

_____

_____

_____

_____

_____

_____

_____

_____

When you finish, take a few deep breaths and exhale. Enjoy the mental space.

Remember, we are all connected.

7

MORNING JOURNALING:

Did you meditate this week?

_____

_____

_____

_____

_____

_____

Did you simplify in any way?

_____

_____

_____

_____

_____

_____

_____

What was the most valuable thing you learned or discovered about yourself this week?

_____

_____

_____

_____

_____

Who oversaw your life this week? Spirit or ego?

_____

_____

_____

_____

_____

What was the most surprising "aha" insight of the week?

_____

_____

_____

_____

_____

INTUITIVE MESSAGE
Always trust your vibes.

DAY

1

Sometimes intuition doesn't flow as quickly or clearly as we would like it to. This doesn't mean your intuition isn't working. More likely your intuition is telling you that you are asking about something too soon. Events may need to develop further before you get an accurate intuitive read on a situation. When you do not get an intuitive answer, you may be at an intuitive "yellow light," encouraging you to pause and wait a little longer before moving forward.

MORNING JOURNALING:

In what area of your life have you asked for but not received clear, intuitive direction? When checking with your heart, do you feel this may be a time to use the power of the pause? What do your vibes say?

_____

_____

_____

When you finish writing, let the question go for today. Let things develop a little more. Ask again in a few days. Review what you wrote. If you are at ease, your spirit is in charge. if you are seeking approval, your barking dog/ego is driving the bus. Who do you want to drive the bus today?

EVENING REFLECTION:

Was today a "red light" vibe day? A "green light" vibe day? Or a "yellow light" vibe day?

_____

_____

_____

_____

_____

_____

_____

_____

_____

_____

_____

_____

_____

_____

_____

When you finish, take a few deep breaths and exhale. The day is over. It's time to rest.

INTUITIVE MESSAGE
Follow the signals.

2

The more you activate your intuition, the more obvious it becomes not to take other people's behavior personally. While others' behavior can affect you, the way they behave is never about you. It is only a reflection of their own spiritual level of awareness and development at any time. Use your intuition and good sense to reject others' negative energy, and to disallow others' limited behaviors or perceptions to cloud your view of yourself.

MORNING JOURNALING:

Is anyone treating you poorly right now, or causing you to doubt yourself? Are you being unfairly projected upon or blamed for what is simply untrue? Are you around people who just don't get you and never will?

_____

_____

_____

_____

_____

_____

_____

_____

Step back and realize it's not you. It is them. Also realize it is important to surround yourself with good people.

EVENING REFLECTION:

Are there any people in your life who are not good for you? These are not necessarily bad people. Just not good for you people. It is okay to acknowledge this.

_____

_____

_____

_____

_____

_____

_____

_____

_____

_____

_____

_____

When you finish, take a few deep breaths and exhale. Release the day and others' energy along with it.

INTUITIVE MESSAGE
It's not about you.

DAY

3

The more you calmly study things and people in detail before responding, the easier it becomes to receive clear, intuitive guidance on that person or situation. Your inner guidance gets scrambled when you get swept up in strong emotions and reactivity. This causes you to misread a situation, draw wrong conclusions, make poor decisions, or go down the wrong path.

MORNING JOURNALING:

Do you study things before you respond? When do you tend to get triggered and react? Who or what triggers you right now?

_____

_____

_____

_____

_____

_____

_____

_____

Using your imagination, observe this person or people in the triggering situation as if they were strangers. Turning on your intuition, ask your spirit to remove your judgments and give you fresh insight into what is happening and why. Ask for better understanding so you can become less reactive and nonjudgmental and move forward in the best possible way.

Quickly write down what your vibes reveal.

_____

_____

_____

Keep this intuitive perspective in mind as you move through the day. The less judgmental and reactive you are, the more intuitively guided and proactive in your life you can be.

EVENING REFLECTION:

How judgmental or reactive to others were you today? What was the best part of the day? How did your vibes help?

_____

_____

_____

_____

_____

_____

_____

_____

_____

When you finish, take a few deep breaths and exhale. Release the day and others' energy along with it.

INTUITIVE MESSAGE
Calmly study and listen.

DAY

4

MORNING VIBE CHECK

Today, vibe check anything you want. First, review the basic vibe check steps, and then you can focus your attention on what it is you're specifically interested in vibe checking.

To begin, take a deep breath through the nose, and then exhale, as if you're blowing out candles, and with it, completely empty everything you are holding on to or that is holding on to you. Repeat this a few times or until your mind feels empty and quiet.

Once you complete this step, close your eyes, turn your attention inward, and slowly scan your area of interest or concern. Be organized. For example, if scanning a person, scan their body, feet to crown. If scanning an event, scan the duration or location of the event. If scanning a potential business decision, scan all people involved. As you scan your concern, notice all subtle energy that calls to your attention. Pay special attention to any energy that feels off-balance, ungrounded, unsafe, misaligned with you, or simply doesn't feel right. Also notice if there is anything about your area of concern that feels particularly positive, warm, connected, uplifting, attractive, fortunate, and appealing. In other words, is this area of concern a positive vibrational match with you? Don't intellectualize or overthink. Simply notice everything you spontaneously sense or feel, however subtle, and trust what comes to mind.

When you sense something, stop, and ask the following questions:

"What is this energy about?" "What can I learn from this?" "How can I correct this?" (if you sense a problem), or "How can I take advantage of this?" (if you sense an opportunity).

Answer quickly with the first thing that enters your mind. Don't try to be logical or justify what you feel, because you won't be able

to. Trust what spontaneously comes to mind, knowing your intuition works perfectly through this method if you relax into it.
Your vibe check revealed:

_____

_____

_____

_____

_____

Stop and occasionally vibe check as you move through your day.

EVENING REFLECTION:

What did your body vibe check advise on your area of concern or interest? Was this a surprise or had you been intuitively feeling it already? What was the happiest part of your day?
Quickly write down everything that comes to mind.

_____

_____

_____

_____

_____

Take a few deep breaths and relax.

INTUITIVE MESSAGE
Vibe check everything and often.

DAY

5

The minute you take a deep breath you come home to your true Self. Breathing deeply quiets your barking dog/ego, grounds your body, opens your heart, and connects you to your inner guidance.

MORNING JOURNALING:

Look around the room, and then turn your attention inward. Notice how you feel. Take your next breath, slowly in through the nose. Then exhale with a loud, deep sigh. Do this one more time. Again, notice how you feel. Pay particular attention to the noise in your head. How has this deep breath affected your barking dog/ego? Next turn your attention to your heart, chest, and stomach area. Slowly inhale and exhale again. Is your heart open or closed after taking another breath? Listen to your spirit. What guidance does it offer now?

_____

_____

_____

_____

_____

_____

When you feel stressed or anxious or you need guidance today, take a deep breath, and then slowly exhale. Smile, and listen to your heart.

EVENING REFLECTION:

Did you remember to breathe deeply today? Were you able to tune into your spirit quickly? What was the best part of the day? How did your intuition help you?

_____

_____

_____

_____

_____

_____

_____

_____

_____

_____

_____

_____

_____

_____

When you finish, take a few deep breaths and exhale. Doesn't that feel good?

INTUITIVE MESSAGE
Breathe some more.

DAY

6

Over the past few months, you've been growing and changing in leaps and bounds. The more you change your perspective from barking dog/ego to conscious, intuitive spirit, the more you will be clearly guided to an extraordinary life. As you grow, so do your values, goals, and intentions. Update your values, goals, and intentions to reflect what is most important to you now.

MORNING JOURNALING:

My top three intentions, priorities, and goals today are:

1 _____

_____

_____

2 _____

_____

_____

3 _____

_____

_____

Ask your spirit and intuition to move you in the direction of your priorities today.

EVENING REFLECTION:

What was your best accomplishment today? What was your biggest intuitive "aha" or download?

_____

_____

_____

_____

_____

_____

_____

_____

_____

_____

_____

_____

_____

When you finish, take a few deep breaths and appreciate how much you've grown.

INTUITIVE MESSAGE
Set your intentions daily.

MORNING JOURNALING:

Did you meditate this week? Drink water? Remember to breathe? Eat well?

_____

_____

_____

_____

_____

What was your greatest intuitive insight this week?

_____

_____

_____

_____

What was the most significant decision you made this week?

_____

_____

_____

_____

_____

What was the most valuable thing you learned or discovered about yourself this week?

_____

_____

_____

_____

_____

Who triggered you most, and how did you respond this week?

_____

_____

_____

_____

_____

What was the most surprising gift you received this week?

_____

_____

_____

_____

_____

_____

INTUITIVE MESSAGE
Always trust your vibes.

DAY

1

The world is changing, and being an openly intuitive person is no longer considered as "weird" as it once was. Rather than harboring ancient fears of rejection and ridicule for listening to your sixth sense, let those fears go and normalize your intuition. Consider it the natural inner compass you comfortably use every day. You'll be surprised at how many people will accept this because they'll see how well-balanced and confident you are, and how wonderfully your life is unfolding.

MORNING JOURNALING:

Are you starting to integrate your intuition as the primary guide in your life? Are your vibes starting to feel as natural to you as your physical senses? Is there anything standing in the way of normalizing your inner guidance system as your natural superpower currently?

_____

_____

_____

_____

_____

Say at least once today, "I trust my vibes because they work for me," with the most natural tone you can manage. Then smile because it's true.

EVENING REFLECTION:

Did you tell anyone today that you trust your vibes because they work for you? What was the biggest gift of the day?

When you finish, take a few deep breaths and appreciate the benefits of giving to give.

INTUITIVE MESSAGE
Trust your vibes because they work for you.

DAY
2

Your intuition is not the enemy of your logical brain. Intuition and logic are designed and intended to be partners, to work together to give you the best possible guidance in life moving forward. However, you must remember that your spirit is the leader, and your logical brain (your barking dog/ego) is the helper. Ideally, your logical brain can be of great support to your intuition by gathering as many accurate, current facts about any decision you face before turning it over to your intuition. Working with a sound foundation of facts, over hearsay, gossip, superstition, outdated information, and secondhand opinion is what matters here. Separate fact from fiction and leave the fiction behind.

MORNING JOURNALING:

Are you able to discern fact from fiction? Can you tell the difference between other people's opinions and the truth of a situation? Do you stop to check?

_____

_____

_____

_____

_____

_____

_____

Take a moment to distinguish between subjective opinion, superstition, and projection from the truth of the situations before you make decisions or formulate opinions of your own today. And then of course, always ask your vibes for guidance.

EVENING REFLECTION:

Did you successfully separate the truth from fiction today? Did this help your intuition work better? Did separating facts from opinion help with your decisions today?

_____

_____

_____

_____

_____

_____

_____

_____

_____

_____

_____

_____

When you finish, take a few deep breaths and appreciate the benefits of giving to give.

INTUITIVE MESSAGE
Seek the truth.

3

Your inner guidance system is natural. What isn't natural is ignoring it, being suspicious of it, doubting it, or casting it aside as something "weird." Reclaim your natural, intuitive superpower, and don't let social conditioning or superstitions steal it from you ever again. Affirm often and out loud, "As a Divine being, I use all of my spiritual gifts, including my intuition, without resistance or question, and give thanks for the blessings they bring." And believe it.

MORNING JOURNALING:

Do you recognize your intuition as a spiritual gift? Is there any past conditioning or superstition keeping you from trusting your vibes?

_____

_____

_____

_____

Create your own affirmation for trusting your vibes and write it below:

_____

_____

_____

_____

Affirmations remove obstacles that steal your power and intuition. Use your personal affirmation daily and reclaim your intuitive power.

EVENING REFLECTION:

Did you use your affirmation today? What was the best part of your day?

_____

_____

_____

_____

_____

_____

_____

_____

_____

_____

_____

_____

_____

_____

INTUITIVE MESSAGE
Affirm your superpower.

MORNING VIBE CHECK:

Today, vibe check anything you want. First, review the basic vibe check steps, and then you can focus your attention on what it is you're specifically interested in vibe checking.

To begin, take a deep breath through the nose, and then exhale, as if you're blowing out candles, and with it, completely empty everything you are holding on to or that is holding on to you. Repeat this a few times or until your mind feels empty and quiet.

Once you complete this step, close your eyes, turn your attention inward, and slowly scan your area of interest or concern. Be organized. For example, if scanning a person, scan their body, feet to crown. If scanning an event, scan the duration or location of the event. If scanning a potential business decision, scan all people involved. As you scan your concern, notice all subtle energy that calls to your attention. Pay special attention to any energy that feels off-balance, ungrounded, unsafe, misaligned with you, or simply doesn't feel right. Also notice if there is anything about your area of concern that feels particularly positive, warm, connected, uplifting, attractive, fortunate, and appealing. In other words, is this area of concern a positive vibrational match with you? Don't intellectualize or overthink. Simply notice everything you spontaneously sense or feel, however subtle, and trust what comes to mind.

When you sense something, stop, and ask the following questions:

"What is this energy about?" "What can I learn from this?" "How can I correct this?" (if you sense a problem), or "How can I take advantage of this?" (if you sense an opportunity).

Answer quickly with the first thing that enters your mind. Don't try to be logical or justify what you feel, because you won't be

able to. Trust what spontaneously comes to mind, knowing your intuition works perfectly through this method if you relax into it.

Your vibe check revealed:

_____

_____

_____

_____

_____

Stop and occasionally vibe check as you move through your day.

EVENING REFLECTION:

What did your body vibe check advise on your area of concern or interest? Was this a surprise or had you been intuitively feeling it already? What was the happiest part of your day?
Quickly write down everything that comes to mind.

_____

_____

_____

_____

_____

_____

Take a few deep breaths and relax.

INTUITIVE MESSAGE
Vibe check everything and often.

DAY

5

The Divine Spirit dwells in the heart of you. It illuminates your way like a light in the dark night. It is your companion, protector, moral compass, and creative genius. Stay centered in your heart and you will always be connected to your spirit, where you will always feel guided, protected, and loved.

MORNING JOURNALING:

How connected are you to your intuition today? Is it something you experience occasionally? Is it something you feel all the time? Are you comfortable with your intuition or are you uncertain?

_____

_____

_____

_____

_____

_____

_____

_____

_____

_____

Today treat your intuition as a sacred gift embedded deep in your heart. It is.

EVENING REFLECTION:

Were you aware of the sacred light in your heart today? How did your spirit help you today?

_____

_____

_____

_____

_____

_____

_____

_____

_____

_____

_____

_____

_____

_____

_____

When you finish, take a few deep breaths and relax.

INTUITIVE MESSAGE
Intuition is a sacred gift.

DAY

6

A perpetually negative or critical point of view prevents you from seeing the truth with your intuitive eye. Like pollution on a window, it clouds, distorts, and blocks the view, making the world seem dark and dreary. Keep your perspective clear by looking at life with appreciation, acceptance, gratitude, interest, and love.

MORNING JOURNALING:

How is your outlook today? Are you critical of yourself or others? Do you generally feel negative, or do you have a brighter outlook? What is most responsible for clouding your view? What must change to clear your outlook?

Did you have a clear outlook today? Or was it overcast? How did your vibes help you today?

Take a few deep breaths and let go of your stress. Open your heart and you will see you are protected.

INTUITIVE MESSAGE
Clear the view.

MORNING JOURNALING:

Did you meditate this week? Drink water? Remember to breathe? Eat well?

_____

_____

_____

_____

What was your greatest intuitive insight this week?

_____

_____

_____

_____

What significant decisions did you make?

_____

_____

_____

_____

_____

What was the most valuable thing you learned or discovered about yourself this week?

_____

_____

_____

_____

_____

Who triggered you, and how did you respond this week?

_____

_____

_____

_____

_____

What was the most surprising gift you received this week?

_____

_____

_____

_____

_____

INTUITIVE MESSAGE
Always trust your vibes.

ABOUT THE AUTHOR

Sonia Choquette is globally renowned as an author, spiritual mentor, intuitive advisor, and catalyst for transformation. Sonia masterfully combines humor and skill to awaken our innate sixth sense, leading to healthier, happier, and more meaningful lives. She has written 28 international bestsellers on intuitive development, personal growth, and creativity, including *Trust Your Vibes*, *Ask Your Guides*, and the *New York Times* bestseller *The Answer is Simple*. With her work published in over 40 countries and translated into 37 languages, she stands out as one of the most widely read and respected authors in her field. Sonia also hosts a weekly podcast, It's All Related: Welcome to the Family.

When not globetrotting, Sonia splits her time between Paris and London. In her leisure hours, she enjoys spending time with her daughters and granddaughter, socializing with friends at cafes, or taking long strolls along the Seine or in London's parks. To learn more about Sonia, please visit soniachoquette.net

HAY HOUSE TITLES OF RELATED INTEREST

YOU CAN HEAL YOUR LIFE, the movie,
starring Louise Hay & Friends
(available as an online streaming video)
www.hayhouse.com/louise-movie

THE SHIFT, the movie,
starring Dr. Wayne W. Dyer
(available as an online streaming video)
www.hayhouse.com/the-shift-movie

***

THE COSMIC JOURNAL, by Yanik Silver

*THE GIFT OF GRATITUDE: A Guided Journal for
Counting Your Blessings,* by Louise Hay

*LIVING YOUR PURPOSE JOURNAL: A Guided Path
to Finding Success and Inner Peace,* by Dr. Wayne W. Dyer

SUPER ATTRACTOR JOURNAL, by Gabrielle Bernstein

THE UNIVERSE HAS YOUR BACK JOURNAL, by Gabrielle Bernstein

All of the above are available at www.hayhouse.co.uk.

***

CONNECT WITH
HAY HOUSE
ONLINE

🌐 hayhouse.co.uk   **f** @hayhouse

📷 @hayhouseuk   🐦 @hayhouseuk

▶ @hayhouseuk   ♪ @hayhouseuk

Find out all about our latest books & card decks • Be the first
to know about exclusive discounts • Interact with our authors
in live broadcasts • Celebrate the cycle of the seasons with us
• Watch free videos from your favourite authors •
Connect with like-minded souls

'*The gateways to wisdom and knowledge
are always open.*'

Louise Hay